Gordon Hayward: The Inspiring Story of One of Basketball's Star Forwards

An Unauthorized Biography

By: Clayton Geoffreys

Table of Contents

Foreword

Since being selected with the 9th overall pick in the 2010 NBA Draft, Gordon Hayward has worked diligently to improve year after year in order to become an All-Star. After seven years with the Utah Jazz, Hayward made the decision to join the Boston Celtics in their pursuit of another championship. It will be fun to see how Hayward and the Celtics do in the years to come as Hayward teams up with Al Horford and Kyrie Irving. Thank you for purchasing *Gordon Hayward: The Inspiring Story of One of Basketball's Star Forwards*. In this unauthorized biography, we will learn Gordon Hayward's incredible life story and impact on the game of basketball. Hope you enjoy and if you do, please do not forget to leave a review!

Also, check out my website at claytongeoffreys.com to join my exclusive list where I let you know about my latest books. To thank you for your purchase, you can go to my site to download a free copy of *33 Life*

Lessons: Success Principles, Career Advice & Habits of Successful People. In the book, you'll learn from some of the greatest thought leaders of different industries on what it takes to become successful and how to live a great life.

Cheers,

Clayton Geoffreys

Visit me at www.claytongeoffreys.com

Introduction

The game of basketball is always a learning process. Nobody in this world is born an expert in the sport, or even someone who has mastered certain skills one way or another. Every superstar and all-time great has gone through periods of learning, training, and developing to become who they are today and who they are in the history of basketball. However, the pace may be somewhat different.

While it is true that superstars and all-time greats have had to undergo the same process that every basketball player has had to go through to become better, there are some who seem like they were born to it. That is where genetics come into play. Though nobody is born a superstar in basketball, some were brought into this world with the pedigree and genetic makeup that would someday make them greats in the game with the proper training, coaching, and development.

The physical aspect is what is initially looked at when it comes to telling how much of a potential a basketball player has. He might be an athletic freak of nature like Wilt Chamberlain, Shaquille O'Neal, and LeBron James are. And some may be genetic miracles because of their size, length, and athleticism. Players such as Giannis Antetokounmpo and Kristaps Porzingis might come to mind.

Oftentimes, a player's destiny as a future star could also be a legacy carried on from one generation to one another. Players that have had parents as basketball players and NBA professionals often have the genetics to someday follow in the footsteps of their forebears. Those that come to mind are Kobe Bryant, Klay Thompson, and Stephen Curry, among others. Such players seemed to have been born with the talent to one day become as great as their fathers or mothers but only through work ethic did they achieve the heights that they reached.

However, there are those that may be born with the height and other physical tools to achieve, but were never as superior genetically or athletically compared to other stars that have played in the NBA. Such players had to work through blood, sweat, and tears to get to where they are. And with enough hard work, they improved their abilities every season. One such player in today's NBA is Gordon Hayward.

Playing two years in a mid-major college such as Butler University, a school never as big or successful as some of the more prominent colleges in the country, Gordon Hayward is regarded as the Bulldogs' most successful basketball player. This is not only because he was able to forge himself a stellar NBA career, but also because of how he led the Butler Bulldogs to an NCAA Finals run that almost gave his team its first-ever national championship.

There were not a lot of expectations on Gordon Hayward when the Utah Jazz drafted him ninth overall in the 2010 NBA Draft. He was playing behind more experienced guards and forwards such as Raja Bell, CJ Miles, and Andrei Kirilenko at that time. He was but a role player and long-term project for a Utah Jazz team that seemed like it was in a middle of a transition period.

As his career went on, Gordon Hayward's role and minutes increased, though his skills were not yet on par with the time he was seeing and possessions he was getting. The Utah Jazz did not see as much success either as they struggled to win even half of their games. But if the Jazz had something to be hopeful of, it was that Gordon Hayward was improving steadily every season.

Gordon Hayward would show improvements to his statistics and skills every season. His numbers would increase, and it was clear that his abilities and body of work were growing. Hayward became a steady scoring and playmaking force for the Utah Jazz until he broke out to become a respectable go-to option on the offensive end during the 2014-15 season. However, it was not until the 2016-17 season when he rose to become an All-Star.

During the 2016-17 season, Gordon Hayward became the established star of the Utah Jazz, who were rising to become one of the best defensive forces in the NBA. While the Jazz were focusing their energy on the defensive end of the floor, Hayward was their most reliable offensive weapon. The Butler product would develop into an exceptional scorer and shooter that led the Jazz to their first 50-win season in a long while. Because of how he was able to turn the Utah Jazz around from a mere eighth seed contender into a 50-win team, he was given his first All-Star berth and the status as one of the best small forwards in the entire NBA.

After that All-Star season, Gordon Hayward became one of the hottest names in free agency because of his versatility at the small forward position. While he contemplated returning to Utah to continue to play for a Jazz team that became patient with him as he worked hard on his skills to develop into an exceptional star, he would decide to join the Boston Celtics. Joining the Celtics meant that he was reuniting with his college coach Brad Stevens, a man that he deeply respected and one of the many reasons as to why he was able to lead the Bulldogs to that NCAA Finals run back in 2010.

As the newest Celtic star, Hayward has a lot of expectations on his shoulder considering that his new team is one of the most storied franchises in the history of the NBA and was just coming off a season where they won the top seed in the Eastern Conference. Joining the likes of offseason acquisition Kyrie Irving and upstart rookie Jayson Tatum, Hayward was not expected to carry the offensive load as heavy as he did back in Utah. Nevertheless, the Butler product is projected to provide the same kind of scoring punch and leadership that helped the Utah Jazz grow steadily to a contender in the seven seasons he spent with them.

Chapter 1: Childhood and Early Life

Gordon Daniel Hayward was born on March 23, 1990, in Indianapolis, Indiana. However, he was not alone. He was born together with twin sister Heather Hayward. The Hayward twins would be raised and grow up in Brownsburg, which is a small town just a few miles away from Indianapolis. Despite being only 18 miles away from Indianapolis, Brownsburg only had a population of about 14,000 back then. But growing up in a basketball-crazy state, it was not difficult to make Gordon love the sport he would soon play for a living.

Indiana is known as one of the states that loves and embraces basketball more than any other country, state, or city in the world. The Indiana University Hoosiers were primarily responsible for the popularity of basketball in the state because of how successful it has been in the NCAA. The Indiana Pacers have also seen their share of basketball success in the NBA and has contributed to how the people of the State have come to love the sport. One can only imagine how easy of task it was for the family to make Gordon Hayward love basketball.

Speaking of family, the father, Gordon Scott Hayward Sr., and the mother, Jody Hayward, were also fans of basketball though they met at a tennis court. The elder Gordon, a software engineer, stood 5'10" and so did his wife Jody, who was also a twin much like the younger Gordon was. Because of their love for basketball, it was easy for the parents to accept the athletic endeavors of not only Gordon, but also of his twin sister Heather.

As early as the age of five, Gordon Hayward was already aiming to one day play in the NBA. At that time, he could not even write, but with the help of his father, he would write the goal of one day becoming a professional basketball player in the NBA. Of course, the little boy had a lot of goals in mind. He had posted all of those goals on a bulletin board in the corner of their home in Brownsburg. But the top of all those goals was playing in the NBA.[i]

Gordon Hayward's road to the NBA was mapped out, and he would check goals off of his list one by one. Some of the core goals he had were to become a starter for his sixth-grade team and to earn significant roles as a contributor for his seventh and eighth-grade squads.[ii] As simple as those goals were, they were major steps for him to someday develop the skills he would need to make it to the NBA, which was the final destination of his childhood aspirations.

But before Gordon Hayward would even start for his sixth-grade team, the first time he would get to play basketball was with his father Gordon Sr. As most children do, the younger Gordon would start with a tiny foam ball and a mini-hoop inside the house. And by the age of four, his father signed him up for an Indianapolis league where the hoops were merely six feet tall and the basketballs were just the right size for four-year-olds.[i]

But even as a child, Gordon Hayward already had the makings of a star. He was a child prodigy. The coach would often tell the other kids to get Gordon the ball. The young Hayward was showing so much skill at his age that the coach would call his name when the scores were already close. After the young Hayward showed so much competitiveness, the league decided to do away with keeping track of the scoring because they realized that such level of competition was too much for four-year-olds.[i]

Gordon Hayward was always competitive as a young boy. He always aimed for victory in everything he tried his hand in. From basketball, football, tennis, video games, and soccer, Gordon Hayward tried his best to excel. He also did well in academics. Pretty soon, he would even start to compete against his twin sister Heather. The twins would compete against each other in tests scores and athletic achievements. But they tried to remain close as much as possible, and it even devastated Gordon when they were put in separate classes in the fourth grade.[iii]

Growing up in a small town meant that Gordon Hayward had a sense of balance in his life. He tried to do it all. Aside from competing against his twin sister in school and athletics, he competed against himself by playing any competitive sport he could find. He was often seen changing uniforms inside the family van when they drove him from one sporting venue to another. And when at home, he tried his hand at strategic video gaming, thinking that he could someday become a competitive gamer and make money out of it. But his father decided to limit his video gaming, telling him that it was not in his future.[iii]

What was in Gordon Hayward's future was, of course, basketball. Before he got to his freshman year in high school, he was standing barely 5'10". Doctors were telling him that he had height ceiling of 6'2". Because of that, his father had him focus on the basics and fundamental skills of a guard. The younger Gordon would practice his ballhandling, outside shooting, and playmaking. And since guards should always be reliable free throw shooters, it was a point of emphasis that he would hone his skills at the charity stripe. Gordon Sr. would wake him up early in the morning to do the Steve Alford free throw shooting drills. He was so fundamentally good as a guard that his youth coaches back then thought he had the makings of a Division I point guard. However, they would be half wrong on that assessment.

Chapter 2: High School Career

Gordon Hayward would attend Brownsburg High School in his hometown. At that point, he was standing 5'11" and was close to reaching his predicted ceiling of 6'2". He was a point guard for the freshman team and was not even selected to be a part of his high school's varsity squad. This led him to nearly quit the game of basketball because he knew he lacked the height to forge a path to the NBA. At 5'11", he would have had a solid high school career and respectable college stint. But he knew he could not make it to the NBA if he could not even get to his ceiling of 6'2".

Luckily for Gordon Hayward, he had a backup plan. He and his sister Heather were competitive tennis players. Before he was called up for the basketball varsity team, he was already a star tennis player. Ever the tight siblings, Gordon and Heather were ruling the court in mixed doubles. This led to Gordon Hayward to dream of winning titles as a tennis player or making a career out of it.

Believing that tennis was his ticket to a college program scholarship and better life, Gordon Hayward would practice daily on how he would tell his junior varsity coach that he planned on quitting basketball.[i] At 5'11", he had the proper height to excel in tennis. Realistically though, he could not excel at basketball with his lack of size. He thought of focusing more on tennis when he was a freshman.

Jody Hayward would intervene. When Gordon Hayward was already preparing himself to quit basketball and focus on tennis because he believed he lacked the size to compete, his mother would push him forward. Jody Hayward would not allow her son to quit basketball because she knew that Gordon loved the sport more than anything else. Gordon Hayward gave in, though he would only give it one more year. If he could not break out in that one-year span, he would focus on playing tennis.[iii]

It turned out that one year was all that Gordon Hayward needed. By his sophomore year, he had made it to the varsity team. He would then also experience a growth spurt that suddenly shot him up from 5'11" to 6'4". He would exceed his predicted ceiling of 6'2". Fortunately, he was also still growing. His father, who was not a very tall man himself, called it a "divine intervention" that Gordon Hayward saw a massive growth spurt.[iv]

While Gordon Sr. would call the growth spurt "a gift from God," high school coach Joshua Kendrick would describe the younger Hayward's overnight transformation as "like a kid discovered superpowers."[iv] It as what saved Gordon Hayward's basketball career because he no longer had to worry about his size to be able to play in more competitive settings.

As a sophomore, Gordon Hayward was a rotation player and was backup for his team. He had not broken out yet, but Red Taylor, who was the coach of the Municipal Garden travel teams, saw that Hayward was a player that had mental quickness and a calm demeanor on the floor. He rarely panicked or did anything out of the ordinary. But the problem with him was that he was always overshadowed by bigger and stronger players. He did not even think that Hayward was going to make it to the NBA.[i]

The best performance that Gordon Hayward had during his sophomore year was during the sectionals. Brownsburg's starting point guard struggled with foul trouble. They also did not have their backup point guard that night. That was when Kendrick had to rely on the 6'4" sophomore Gordon Hayward to play the point guard position. He took over that night and showed flashes of what he could someday be.[i] While Kendrick also initially thought that Hayward would not make it to the NBA, he certainly changed his mind that night. He was impressed by his sophomore guard's vision and ability to make plays for others.

The growth spurt did not stop. During the summer before his junior year, Gordon Hayward was already 6'6". The former point guard had transformed into a player with the height of a swingman. Hayward had turned into a unique player. He played the small forward position but could handle and shoot the ball like a guard. Luckily for him, his athleticism would also cooperate with his growth spurt.

It was the summer before his junior year when Gordon Hayward made his first ever in-game slam dunk. He had never dunked in practices or games. He was always a player that liked shooting from the perimeter or making shots under the basket. However, he wowed his teammates when he caught the ball during the transition and dunked it with his left hand. The bench went crazy, especially because they were seeing how much their teammate was improving at the same rate his height was growing.

Unfortunately, Gordon Hayward would suffer a broken wrist before his junior year. That was one of the biggest reasons why he went under the radar that season when college programs started their recruitment process. Hayward was hardly gaining attention from Division I schools, though he had a decent year as a starting swingman for Brownsburg. He averaged 13.6 points and was a secondary player that season.

Before his senior year, Gordon Hayward would attend a workout for the top 100 juniors of Indiana. That was when he garnered attention after having fallen out of the radar of most recruiters during his junior year. Hayward performed better than expected during that workout and impressed then-Butler University head coach Brad Stevens. Stevens would go to Brownsburg shortly after that and would ask the coach not to expose the junior so much in the leagues that summer out of fear that all the other programs would want to recruit him. At that point, Brad Stevens even thought that Gordon Hayward was good enough to make the NBA.

During his senior year, Gordon Hayward would shoot up to 6'8", and his height had matured to what was needed of him to play the small forward position in Division I basketball and probably even in the NBA. That was the year when he finally broke out to become the top man in Brownsburg. He would often hear coaches urging his teammates to give him the ball. The last time he heard that was when he was still four years old.

Gordon Hayward's signature moment in his senior year was during the important 4A state title game. Gordon Hayward was the target during an inbound play when Brownsburg was down a point with only 2.1 seconds remaining. When the play was botched and the ball was loose in the lane, Hayward grabbed it and converted the layup to give his team the win and to give the Brownsburg Bulldogs their first-ever state title. During that season, Hayward was named First Team All-State after averaging 18 points, 8.4 rebounds, and 3.6 assists.

Considered an all-around player rather than a scorer, Gordon Hayward did not even finish high school as Brownsburg's all-time leading scorer. He did not even crack 1,000 career points, though he ranked high in rebounds, assists, and steals. Nevertheless, he was considered one of their best products after being the one to deliver the school's first-ever state title.

In high school, Gordon Hayward would receive three college basketball scholarships. The three programs interested in him were IUPUI, Purdue, and Butler. His choices boiled down to either Purdue or Butler. Both of his parents were Purdue alums. He grew up as a fan of Purdue because of his parents. However, the basis of his choice was something outside of basketball.

Gordon Hayward would accept Brad Stevens' offer to go to Butler, but not because he thought the program was better. Wanting to major in computer engineering much like his father, a software engineer, Hayward liked the idea of early morning practices because it would not interfere with his classes. His sister was also on his mind. Heather was a tennis star who was also offered a scholarship in Butler. Not wanting to part ways from his twin sister, Gordon Hayward chose Butler so that he could play basketball while Heather could compete in tennis. While Hayward was also a tennis star in high school, he would ultimately commit everything he had to basketball when he attended Butler.

Chapter 3: College Career

Freshman Season

Brad Stevens was ecstatic about having Gordon Hayward on his team. Butler University was never the most successful college program. As a mid-major school, Butler could hardly recruit great basketball talents that could take the basketball world by storm. They would even struggle to produce players good enough to make it all the way to the NBA. However, Stevens was confident. He believed that what Butler had in Gordon Hayward was the school's first NBA player in six decades. That was saying a lot considering that Butler did not have a lot of NBA players in its history.[iii]

Brad Stevens was not shy about how good he thought Gordon Hayward was. He told Gordon Sr. that the younger Gordon was going to be good enough to take his talents to the next level of basketball. While Stevens was not good enough to make it to the NBA during his playing days, he knew talent when he saw it. And with him believing in Hayward, the Butler Bulldogs' freshman was on his way to realizing the childhood dream he has always had—to make it to the NBA.

However, even Hayward's parents were not completely buying into the idea that Gordon was good enough. Jody would ask Stevens if her son was going to be a productive player for the Bulldogs. She thought that the younger Hayward was only going to be a role player off the bench. Meanwhile, Gordon Sr. contemplated having his son redshirting the freshman season.[ii] Little did they know that Gordon Hayward was going to be a freshman standout.

Gordon Hayward had a great start to his college basketball career. In a loss to Ohio State University on December 13, 2008, in one of his first games, he would go for 25 points on 7 out of 11 shooting from the three-point area. He followed that up with a win in

Xavier by going for 19 points and ten rebounds on December 23. In his first game of 2009, he would go for 15 points and 13 rebounds in a win against Valparaiso. Five days later, he had 12 points and 11 rebounds against Wright in a win.

On January 17 in a win against UIC, Gordon Hayward would go for 25 points in another game where he made seven three-pointers. The next time he would go for at least 20 points was on February 2 against Green Bay. He went for 22 points and seven rebounds that night. In the game after that, he would go for 22 points and six rebounds against Detroit.

On March 10, however, Gordon Hayward would only score 7 points against Cleveland State during the Horizon League Tournament Finals. Cleveland State would win that game though Butler was still able to get to the NCAA as a ninth seed. In the round of 64, Hayward had 12 points, six rebounds, and four assists in an elimination loss to LSU.

In his freshman season, Gordon Hayward averaged 13.1 points, 6.5 rebounds, 2.0 assists, and 1.5 steals. He made an immediate impact as a freshman and would win the Horizon League Newcomer of the Year. Brad Stevens' prediction of Hayward becoming an NBA player was not so farfetched. He was the second-leading scorer and rebounder of the team while leading all Bulldogs in steals. He even shot 45% from the three-point line.

Sophomore Season

Gordon Hayward was so good during his rookie season and also in his stint with Team USA in the 2009 FIBA Under-19 World Championship that his stock rose before the 2009-10 season. He would be named as one of the possible candidates for the Wooden and Naismith Awards, which are considered two of the best individual accolades in college basketball. And with the way he and Brad Stevens led a Butler team that nobody even thought would compete the last year, Hayward was predicted to lead the Bulldogs to a better outing during the 2009-10 season.

On November 14, Hayward would go for 17 points and eight rebounds in Butler's opening game that season against Davidson. Then, in a win four days later, he would go for 14 points, ten rebounds, and four assists versus Northwestern. He would cap off a three-game winning start with 15 points and six rebounds against Evansville on November 21.

Gordon Hayward would have his first game of scoring at least 20 points on December 8 against Georgetown. Despite the loss, he had 24 points and eight rebounds in that performance. He followed that up four days later with 24 points and eight rebounds in a win over Ohio State. He had 22 points and 14 rebounds versus Xavier after that. Butler was 8-4 at that point of the season.

On December 31, Gordon Hayward would help Butler win the first of what was to become a 25-game winning streak for the Bulldogs. One of his best games during that run was on February 4, 2010, when he had 18 points and ten rebounds in a win versus Detroit. A week later, he would go for 22 points and 17 rebounds against Youngstown. He continued in the next four games with four more double-doubles as the Butler Bulldogs continued to win.

On March 9, Gordon Hayward would score 8 points when the Bulldogs did not even need his production to beat Wright in the Horizon League Tournament finals. With a record of 28 wins as against only four losses, Butler made it to the NCAA Tournament as a fifth seed. Their miracle run would continue throughout the entire tournament.

On March 18 against UTEP in the Round of 64, Gordon Hayward had 13 points, four rebounds, and four assists in a win. He would then go for 12 points and seven rebounds in the second round when Butler defeated Murray State. Then against Syracuse in the Sweet 16, Hayward had 17 points and five rebounds in a four-point win. Butler would then tally win number 23 in the Elite Eight against Kansas State. Gordon Hayward had 22 points and nine rebounds in that game. He would then power the Bulldogs against Michigan State with 19 points and nine rebounds to make it all the way to the NCAA Finals.

In the national championship game, Butler and Duke fought hard to a near stalemate. Neither team wanted to give an inch. But the Blue Devils got the advantage when there were mere seconds left on the clock. Channeling the player that made the game-winning shot two years ago in Indiana, Gordon Hayward heaved a half-court shot when the time expired. The shot had a good line and would hit the backboard. However, the ball would not make its goal. Had it done so, Hayward would have been a hero all over again and would have given Butler their first-ever NCAA title.

Despite finishing the season as a runner-up, Gordon Hayward had already done everything he needed to do to convince NBA scouts about his stock. He led the Butler Bulldogs to a miracle run towards the NCAA Finals though nobody even gave that mid-major team its due. Nobody expected the Bulldogs to even make a dent in the NCAA Tournament. But thanks to Hayward, they became a crowd favorite. The Indiana product would average 15.5 points, 8.2 rebounds, and 1.7 assists that season. He would win the Horizon League Player of the Year award as well as the West Region MVP award during the NCAA Tournament.

After that season, Gordon Hayward would decide to move on from college to fulfill his NBA dreams. Brad Stevens supported his decision knowing full well that he was going to have a long and productive NBA career because of his talents, ability to win games, and mental focus on what he needed to do. Although his parents would make it a difficult decision, Hayward would announce on April 10, 2010, that he was nearly done with his childhood list of goals. The only thing he needed to do was go to the NBA.

Hayward would leave Butler as arguably the best product the program has produced in a long while. He was going to be a sure pick in the NBA as Brad Stevens' prediction was about to come true. More importantly, the four-year-old Gordon Hayward would have been proud to see his 20-year-old self joining the 2010 NBA Draft as a sure first-round pick. While his parents only made him write that NBA dream to teach him the importance of setting goals, the only question they only needed to answer was how high in the draft would Gordon Hayward go.

Chapter 4: NBA Career

Getting Drafted

The 2010 NBA Draft was a class that had several talented players would soon become All-Stars. The draft class' consensus top pick was Kentucky point guard John Wall because of his unimaginable athleticism and ability to play the point guard position at a high level. Evan Turner was also considered a highly-touted prospect and would have a productive NBA career. The draft also featured two other future All-Stars in Kentucky center DeMarcus Cousins and Fresno State swingman Paul George.

As draft day was nearing, the consensus top small forward in that class was Wesley Johnson of Syracuse. Al-Farouq Aminu of Wake Forest was also considered a lottery pick as a small forward. However, none of those players would have a career as good as Gordon Hayward's, though the Butler product would be drafted below those two other small forwards.

Coming into the 2010 NBA Draft, Gordon Hayward had a good height for a small forward. He was measured standing 6'8", but some would say that he would grow one more inch to come close to 6'9". He was not also so skinny though his appearance may say otherwise. He weighed about 211 pounds. Athletically, he could do well with a vertical leap of about 35 inches. He also moved deceptively quickly and could control his body well.[v]

Offensively, it was Gordon Hayward's ability to hit perimeter jumpers that got a lot of attention. As a shooter, Hayward has a quick and high enough release that it makes it difficult for defenders to contest his shots. At nearly 6'9", he could also shoot over smaller defenders with ease. And with his smooth mechanics and fluid form, he would be able to contribute well in the NBA if his role boiled down to being an outside shooter.

Gordon Hayward's ability to hit the jumper was not merely a product of catch-and-shoot situations. Back at Butler, he could hit pull-up jump shots from the perimeter. And among all small forwards in the draft class, he had the highest conversation rate of shots within the perimeter because not only could he hit pull-up jumpers but he could also hit contested ones. And with an array of step-back moves and crossover dribbles, Hayward could get enough space to manufacture shots from the perimeter.[v]

Gordon Hayward was also never a one-trick pony on the offensive end. Relying on his ability to get to the basket, he uses his underrated athleticism and excellent body control to attack the rim and draw fouls, which he converts at an insanely high rate for a small forward. While he may not be the strongest or most explosive player, he has a good touch around the basket to be able to make layups and conversions inside the lane.

Gordon Hayward has also shown promise as a ball handler. Though he may play the small forward spot, Hayward can handle the ball exceptionally well for his size because of his training as a guard when he was a young boy. He does not wow anyone with slick handles that could break defenses down, but he could do well enough with his dribbling skills to get to the basket or create separation for himself. With his high basketball IQ and mental understanding of the game, Hayward could also make the right passes at the right time while also making sure that his teammates were in the best available spots.

As a rebounder, Gordon Hayward was able to collect a lot of rebounds using his size. He uses his basketball IQ well enough to know where the ball bounces during a missed shot. That was why he was able to get a lot of offensive rebounds for a small forward. And with his athleticism, he could also get up there to challenge bigger players for the boards.

Being as smart as he is, Gordon Hayward knows how to defend properly and can even get intense and physical when guarding his man. His understanding of the game helps him get his hands on the passing lanes for steals. His vertical leap and respectable length also help him contest shots at the perimeter or near the basket when he switched to the power forward spot back in college. On a mental aspect, his defensive mechanics are excellent. He does not overcommit, stays with the play, and always tries to understand the limitations and tendencies of his defensive assignment.

While Hayward may have a lot of upsides on the offensive end as a shooter, he did have a lot of weaknesses in his game. This led to scouts believing that other small forwards such as Wesley Johnson and Al-Farouq Aminu had higher chances of getting drafted in the lottery. Not a lot of scouts were raving about his potential as a future star because of the weaknesses he brought with him to the NBA.

Physically, though Gordon Hayward had the height to shoot over defenders, he was always a skinny kid. He lacked the bulk and strength to bump bodies with bigger players inside the lane or to muscle his way to foul shot opportunities. Defensively, he may have a problem matching up with the larger and more physical small forwards like LeBron James and Carmelo Anthony because he does not have enough strength and muscle to stay on them for too long.

While Gordon Hayward may be deceptively fast and athletic, he does not have the lateral quickness to become a solid defender.[v] His defensive mechanics and aggression are already there, especially from a mental standpoint. However, Hayward might find it too difficult of a task to guard quick perimeter players if he ever got matched up with guards and other speedy wings. He might struggle in defending dribble penetration because of the limitations on his lateral movement. Putting him up against slower but bigger players would also be a problem because of his lack of heft and strength.

On the offensive end, Gordon Hayward does not always get to the rim as much as he needs to. While he may be called on by his team to shoot baskets from the perimeter, he may struggle when defenses close out hard on him because of his lack of a dribble penetration game. Despite the fact that he has handles that are better than what most small forwards have, Hayward does not always use them to his advantage when trying to get to the basket.

While he was a good shooter, there were also questions about his catch-and-shoot abilities. As a freshman, he was an excellent shooter off the catch because defenses were not closing out on him. During his sophomore season, however, Brad Stevens revolved the offense around him. He became more of a creator than a catch-and-shoot player. As the top option on offense, his numbers were terrible when defenses were giving him attention. He lost his groove as a catch-and-shoot player. Considering that he might not be ready to become a creator in the NBA, teams might be wary that he might not translate into a deadly set shooter in the professional leagues.

Because of his ability to stretch defenses with his shooting, Gordon Hayward was often a matchup problem when he was in Butler. His mobility and dribbling skills could make it a difficult task for forwards to keep up with him while guards might not be long enough to contest his shots. However, the problem with Hayward was that he had no post game, which would have made him the perfect matchup nightmare. When guarded by smaller defenders, he often opted to shoot over them than trying to post them up. Had he been a much better post player, Gordon Hayward's stock would have significantly improved coming into the draft.

Mentally, the biggest knock on Hayward's game was his lack of aggression and killer instinct. He has the shooting skills and an excellent array of offensive moves that could make him a much better scorer than he was in high school and college. However, he often made it a point to defer to his teammates more often than he should have. That was why he was never a high profile scorer. He could not dominate games when he was needed to, though Brad Stevens relied on him for the bulk of the offense during college. With that kind of a mindset, it was hard to project Gordon Hayward as the centerpiece of an offense. At best, scouts thought that he would probably be a glorified version of a Mike Dunleavy Jr. or the American counterpart of a Hedo Türkoğlu.

When draft day came, John Wall was selected the top overall pick to nobody's surprise. The top wing player picked up was Evan Turner at the second overall spot. Wesley Johnson, the fourth pick, was the first small forward taken. Al Farouq Aminu was then taken at the eighth spot. At number nine, the Utah Jazz had a tough choice to make.

At that time, the Utah Jazz was a consistent playoff team that would always fall at the hands of other contenders such as the LA Lakers and the San Antonio Spurs among others. The fanbase hoped that they would take a big man that could contend with the likes of Pau Gasol and Tim Duncan in the paint considering that their perimeter was already covered All-Star Deron Williams and mainstays Andrei Kirilenko and Raja Bell. Everyone thought they were one big man away from contention.

Holding a lottery pick, which was rare for a then consistent Jazz franchise at that time, Utah still had a lot of choices as far as big men were concerned. Shot blockers Cole Aldrich, Ed Davis, and Larry Sanders were still available. Kevin Séraphin from France also had the heft to be able to bang with gigantic big men. Then there was also Patrick Patterson, a versatile and proven big man from Kentucky. The Jazz even tried to trade up to nab DeMarcus Cousins, who the Kings took with the fifth pick. However, none of that came to fruition. Utah had other plans.

When the Jazz could not trade up for Cousins, fans thought they were going to draft a big man. Instead, then general manager Kevin O'Connor went a different direction by selecting the man he thought was the best available prospect. He would take Gordon Hayward to the dismay of several fans and experts.[vi] While Hayward was not ready to be a steady contributor, O'Connor believed that he had made the right decision, though Paul George, who was picked after him, turned out to be arguably the best player of the class.

Indiana would pick after Utah and selected Paul George. Gordon Hayward would have wanted to trade places with George because Indiana was home to him and was where he developed his love for basketball. Though he had dreamed of always playing for the

Pacers, he was more than happy just to be given a chance to play in the NBA. And knowing how hard the Utah Jazz play, Hayward was excited about working just as hard as his teammates do.

While it was still difficult to gauge whether Utah made the right choice of drafting Hayward, the fact was that the Butler standout had already fulfilled his Indiana childhood goal of making it to the NBA. Being an NBA player was at the top of his list. He never thought of any other plans that would follow after making it to the NBA. But now that his end goal was fulfilled, Hayward was on his way to writing new plans for himself and what he could do to help the Utah Jazz.

Rookie Season

Coming into his rookie season, there were not a lot of expectations on Gordon Hayward. While some young players drafted high were regarded as long-term projects that needed years of development before becoming stars, Hayward was not one of them.

Nobody truly saw the potential he had to become a star. He was a productive and skilled player that had what it took to be a good one in the NBA. But Hayward, with his moppy hair and boyish looks, was not a player with hidden super-talents waiting to tapped. The best that anyone could project of him was that he would be a glorified role player. But Hayward would eventually prove expectations wrong. But everything starts somewhere. Gordon Hayward's work towards becoming a star would start during his rookie season.

As a rookie, Gordon Hayward was not expected to be a big difference-maker to the Utah Jazz. The Jazz had won 53 games the previous year by relying on the famed Jerry Sloan pick-and-roll play of Deron Williams and Carlos Boozer, who were both flanked by productive players in Mehmet Okur and Andrei Kirilenko. They also had role players such as Raja Bell, Paul Milsap, and CJ Miles. However, Boozer would move on while Bell and Okur were getting older. While Williams was still in his prime, they would learn how to rely more on Milsap, Miles, and new acquisition Al Jefferson for the bulk of the scoring. Utah had a lot of weapons on their roster. This left Gordon Hayward in a peculiar spot as a mere role player waiting for his chance to shine.

The first ever Butler Bulldog drafted in the first round of the NBA would make his professional debut on October 27, 2010, in a road game against the Denver Nuggets. Playing 21 minutes off the bench, Gordon Hayward scored 9 points and had five rebounds in his first ever NBA game. The Jazz would lose that one, however. The day after that, he made his debut in front of the Utah crowd. In 25 minutes, he had 6 points, six rebounds, and three blocks in another loss against the Phoenix Suns.

Playing against star Kevin Durant and the Oklahoma City Thunder on October 31, Gordon Hayward had his first taste of NBA victory. He would go for 4 points in only 15 minutes of play in that one. After that, he would see his minutes drop like flies going through bug spray. Gordon Hayward was used sparingly by the Utah Jazz early on. And when he did see time, his role on offense was close to zero. There were a lot of stretches where he would go for no points at all. And if he did score, it would be off of a single field goal only.

On December 29 against the Los Angeles Clippers, Gordon Hayward would get a chance to start for the Utah Jazz, who were without both Andrei Kirilenko and CJ Miles that night. Playing 43 minutes with minimal rest for a Jazz team that lacked depth at the small forward spot that game, Gordon Hayward broke out and had his first double-digit scoring performance. He had 17 points on 6 out of 12 shooting from the field in that win against the Clippers. He also added six rebounds and three assists. He carried the momentum of that game in his next two outings. He would go for 11 markers in a loss to Portland the day after. And starting the year off right, he had 13 points in a win over the Memphis Grizzlies on January 1, 2011.

The Utah Jazz got their regulars back, and Gordon Hayward was relegated to the bench once more. The next time he would score in double digits was on January 21 in a loss to the Boston Celtics. He had 11 points, five rebounds, and three assists in that game. He then had 10 points on a perfect 4 for four shooting night on February 2 in a loss to the Houston Rockets. He would score in double digits a second time in February when he had 14 points on 5 out of 5 shooting from the floor in a loss to the Phoenix Suns 12 days later.

At that time, the Utah Jazz seemed like they were a franchise in trouble just a year after being a consistent 50-win squad. Deron Williams was the only player productive enough to help his team win games. But he had enough. Williams wanted the Utah Jazz to give him some help. He could not get it from Millsap and Jefferson. Gordon Hayward, the rookie, was not good enough to give the point guard the help he wanted, either. Deron Williams would then demand a trade elsewhere.

In what was then seen as a blockbuster move, the Utah Jazz pulled the plug on Williams. They would trade him to the New Jersey Nets in exchange for spitfire point guard Devin Harris and rookie big man Derrick Favors, who was drafted as the third overall pick back in June 2010. With the trade, the Jazz were able to cover all that they needed to do. They got rid of a disgruntled star and replaced him with a productive point guard of the same age. They were then able to cover their frontcourt needs by acquiring a big strong young power forward and center in Derrick Favors. With that move, the Jazz would jumpstart a rebuilding process primarily centered on their rookies Hayward and Favors.

After the trade was pulled, Gordon Hayward would see more minutes for a Utah Jazz team that was hoping they could do well enough with the young pieces that they had. Hayward would eclipse his career high in points on March 11 against the Minnesota Timberwolves in a loss. He finished that game with 18 points after going 6 for eight from the field and a perfect 5 of 5 from the three-point area. He would pass that performance three more times as the season was nearing its end.

On April 3 against the Sacramento Kings, Gordon Hayward would put the team on his back and lead them in minutes in that loss. In 40 minutes of action, he had 19 points on 8 out of 14 shooting from the floor. He eclipsed that mark two days later. Against no less than Kobe Bryant himself, who is legendary for having one of the best midrange games in NBA history, Gordon Hayward outplayed the Black Mamba. Showcasing his midrange abilities, he would make 9 of his 14 shots to score 22 points on top of 6 rebounds and five assists off the bench. It was his defense that was remarkable that night.

Proving that he was not a defensive liability like his pre-draft scouting reports said, Gordon Hayward put the clamps on Kobe Bryant that night. Against the man regarded as one of the best pure scorers in the entire NBA, the skinny rookie out of Butler used his smarts and mental focus by staying in front of Bryant all night long without biting on the legendary guard's fakes and hesitations. His length bothered Bryant to 6 out of 18 shooting as Hayward outplayed the man that would later tutor him in his game. Gordon Hayward's defense was the deciding factor in that win.

That game against the Lakers and Bryant was not the icing on the cake on Gordon Hayward's run at the end of the season. In the final game of the Utah Jazz, Hayward would shoot the lights out of the EnergySolutions Arena in Utah by going for 34 big points to eclipse his career high by 12 points. He made 12 of his 17 attempts from the floor, 5 of his six three-pointers, and all five of his free throws that night to help win the game for the Jazz.

At the end of the regular season, Gordon Hayward averaged 5.4 points on a 48.5% shooting clip from the floor and a 47% three-point shooting accuracy. He may not have had a good rookie season, but Hayward had a productive outing when the Jazz learned how to use him later after the Deron Williams trade. Hayward's accuracy from the field also showed how efficient he was in the touches and the scoring opportunities he got. He converted well enough of his attempts that, had he been given more plays and minutes, he would have scored more for his team.

Gordon Hayward also translated well into the NBA as a spot up shooter for the Utah Jazz. He did well playing as a spacer in a pick-and-roll heavy system that Jerry Sloan loved to use. Whenever the ball found him, he converted it from the perimeter. However, Hayward thought that he should not be contented with being a spot-up shooter. With Deron Williams gone and with Devin Harris unable to repeat his All-Star season, the Butler product realized that he had to improve his handles so that he could open up his game by being able to break defenses down and getting to wherever he wanted to go on the floor. He wanted to be more than just a shooter. Because of that, he would decide to work on his ball-handling skills.

The Steady Rise of Gordon Hayward

The Utah Jazz would add more youth and depth to their lineup during the offseason. They would draft Enes Kanter with the third overall pick they secured in that Deron Williams trade. And with their pick, they selected swingman Alec Burks. Not to fill the roster with young players, they would add veteran Josh Howard via free agency. The Jazz would also replace the retired Jerry Sloan with a hardworking coach in Tyrone Corbin. But shortly after the free agency market, the NBA would enter a lockout that prevented teams from meeting and practicing.

Despite the lockout, Gordon Hayward knew he had to get better with or without his teammates. As the rest of the NBA was sleeping and engaging in talks between the owners and players, other players were getting better on their own. This included Gordon Hayward, who went home to Indianapolis to train at St. Vincent Sports Performance.[vii]

During the offseason in Indiana, Gordon Hayward spent time working on his body. Always known as a skinny baby-faced boy, the former Butler Bulldog would pump iron and lift weights to make himself stronger and bulkier in preparation for another rough grind in the NBA. Not wanting to slow down and get quickly gassed with the added weight, he also worked on his conditioning.

Gordon Hayward also spent time working with new teammate Alec Burks, who practiced on his shooting and strength. While Burks was working on other aspects of his game, Hayward trained hard to improve his ball handles like he promised he would. Knowing that he might start at either the shooting guard or small forward spot and knowing that Utah would need another ball handler without Williams, Hayward predicted that he would have the ball in his hands a lot of time, particularly since Corbin would want to explore mismatches with him on the floor.[vii]

During that offseason training, many would start to describe Gordon Hayward as a perfectionist that worked hard on his game. He did not come into the NBA with the talent level and athleticism that some of his peers have. He also did not have limitless potential. Instead, he would make up for what he lacks by working harder than every other player in the league. Known as a person with several other interests, Hayward pushed all those aside to become a single-minded devotee to improving himself on the court as a basketball player.[vii] He was out there to become a game-changer rather than simply being a role player for the Jazz.

The season would start late in December of 2011 when the lockout ended shortly before that. On December 27 in the Jazz's season debut, they went up against the Lakers. Hayward could not repeat the defensive masterpiece he put on Kobe in their last meeting and ended up falling. He had 8 points in a blowout loss against Los Angeles.

On December 30, to end what was an eventful 2011 for Gordon Hayward, the sophomore swingman would go for his then-season high of 15 points on 5 out of 9 shooting from the field against the Philadelphia 76ers to help give the Jazz their first win of the season. It would take no time for Gordon Hayward to eclipse his season high.

On January 7, 2012, in the middle of what was to become five straight wins for the Utah Jazz, Gordon Hayward had 18 points, six rebounds, four assists, and two steals in a win against the Golden State Warriors. He would outdo that performance eight days later in a win over the Denver Nuggets. Hayward hit 7 of his 13 shots from the floor to score 19 points, his new season high.

Gordon Hayward would exceed that performance once more. Despite a rough start to the season, he would begin seeing traction in that win against the Sacramento Kings. Hayward would hit 7 of his 15 shots to score 21 points in addition to the five rebounds, four assists, and two steals he got on that January 28 game. Five days later, he had the same production in a loss to the Warriors. He hit 6 of his 11 shots to score 21 points in that game.

On February 12, Gordon Hayward had a new season high when the Utah Jazz defeated the Memphis Grizzlies. He hit 8 of his 12 shots from the floor, 2 of his three three-pointers, and all five of his free throws to score 23 points in addition to collecting five rebounds for the Utah Jazz. Because of performances like those, Gordon Hayward was selected to the Rising

Stars Challenge a year after he was snubbed when he was still a rookie.

In a new format where rookies and sophomore were drafted into different teams, Gordon Hayward helped Team Chuck defeat Team Shaq by scoring 17 points off the bench in the Rising Stars Challenge during the All-Star Weekend. That was Hayward's first trip to the All-Star festivities, but would certainly be not his final one as his career progressed.

On March 5, Gordon Hayward would tie his season high against a struggling Cleveland Cavaliers team. In that game, he would make 8 of his 11 shots, 2 of his three three-pointers, and hit all five of his free throws to score 23 points. He also added four rebounds and five assists to his name that night. The Utah Jazz, who were surprisingly good that season, went on to win that game. Gordon Hayward would eclipse his season high once more. In a win over the Minnesota Timberwolves on March 15, the former Bulldog would hit 9 of his 17 shots from the floor to score 26 points.

Gordon Hayward continued to become better and more consistent. On March 28, he would start what was to become a then-personal best nine-game streak of double-digit scoring. He had 19 points, seven rebounds, and five assists in that loss to the Celtics. Then, on April 4, he would go for his first career double-double 20-10 game after going for 20 points and ten rebounds in a loss to the Phoenix Suns. He capped that nine-game run by going for a new season high of 29 points on 9 out of 14 shooting from the field and 4 out of 5 from the three-point line in that win against the Houston Rockets. Gordon Hayward averaged 18.1 points, 5.2 rebounds, and 3.1 assists in that run. He also scored at least 20 points three times.

In his final seven games of the season, Hayward would score in double digits in five of those outings. His best one was when he had 24 points, four rebounds, and five assists against the Dallas Mavericks on April 16. He followed that up with 23 points on 8 out of 11 shooting from the floor against the Portland Trailblazers. He would power the Jazz to win the final five games of the season to help the Jazz qualify for the playoffs as the eighth seed in a competitive Western Conference.

After helping the Utah Jazz win 36 of their 66 games in a lockout-shortened season, Gordon Hayward averaged 11.8 points, 3.5 rebounds, and 3.1 assists while starting for 58 games. He stayed healthy and played all of the Jazz's games that season to be the only player on the roster to have done so. He was also third behind Al Jefferson and Paul Millsap in scoring for the Jazz, who relied on their frontcourt for points.

Gordon Hayward would make his playoff debut on April 29 against the San Antonio Spurs. Fighting against a team that was primed to compete for the NBA title, Hayward had 17 points in what turned out to be a devastating loss for the Jazz. The entire series was one-sided as the Spurs would sweep the Utah Jazz out of the first round. But despite the quick exit, Hayward added another accomplishment to his name. He was finally able to make the playoffs after sitting at home to watch it the past year.

Coming into the 2012-13 season, the Utah Jazz kept their core of Jefferson, Millsap, and Hayward. They would then add veteran combo guards Mo Williams and Randy Foye and defensive forward Marvin Williams. With Marvin Williams in the mix, Ty Corbin decided to relegate Gordon Hayward back to the bench as their designated sixth man while starting the defensive-minded forward in his place.

Gordon Hayward started the season with 11 points in a blowout win against the Dallas Mavericks in the Jazz's home opener for the 2012-13 season. He would score the next three games in double digits and capped the run off with 19 points on 9 out of 17 shooting from the floor in a loss to the Memphis Grizzlies on November 5, 2012.

Easing into his role as the Jazz's sixth man, Hayward would go for 23 points on 8 out of 16 shooting from the field and 9 out of 9 from the free throw line in a win against the Sacramento Kings on November 23, though he was playing off the bench. The next time he would crack 20 points or more was on December 1 in a loss to the Houston Rockets. He was 8 out of 12 from the floor to score 21 points in that one.

One of Gordon Hayward's best games early on was on December 12. The third-year forward from Butler would help lead his team to a win against the highly-favored San Antonio Spurs by going for 19 points, seven rebounds, and six assists in that contest. He made half of his 14 shots from the floor and 4 of the six three-pointers he put up that night as the main gun off the bench for the Utah Jazz.

On December 28, Hayward would start what would become an eight-game stretch of double-digit scoring. He began by scoring 17 points against the LA Clippers by living at the free throw line. His best outing during that run was when he had 27 points against the Dallas Mavericks on January 7, 2013. He was 8 out of 15 from the field and 4 out of 5 from the three-point line in that game. During that run, Hayward averaged 16.4 points on a 55% shooting clip from the three-point area.

Just when Gordon Hayward was getting going, he would meet a setback on January 26 against the Indiana Pacers. Hayward would injure his right shoulder against his hometown team and would have to miss nine games because of it. Nevertheless, he still had 15 points off the bench when the Utah Jazz defeated the Pacers that night.

Gordon Hayward returned to the lineup better than he was before the injury as if he did not miss a beat. In his return game on February 19, he would go for 17 points on 5 out of 9 shooting in a win over the Golden State Warriors. He followed that up with 23 points and eight rebounds in a loss to the Clippers. He then went for 26 points against the Boston Celtics on February 25 to cap off a three-game scoring run after returning from injury.

On March 20, Gordon Hayward matched his season high by going for 27 points in addition to the eight rebounds he collected. In that loss to the Houston Rockets, he made 9 of his 15 shots from the floor, 3 of his four three-pointers, and 6 of his eight free throws. Hayward also added eight rebounds to his name in that contest. That game was the tail end of what was a six-game double-digit scoring run for Gordon Hayward.

When the 2012-13 season concluded, Gordon Hayward once again increased his scoring numbers. He averaged 14.1 points, 3.1 rebounds, and 3.0 assists. Hayward also shot 41% from the three-point line to showcase how deadly a marksman he was. He appeared in 72 games and started in just 27 of them. However, he would not get any consideration for the Sixth Man of the Year award despite his improved production as the first man off the bench of the Utah Jazz.

The Utah Jazz that season were again over .500 concerning wins. They won 43 games against 39 losses. But playing in the Western Conference meant that they had to perform better than that to make the playoffs. The Jazz would miss the postseason just a year after making it for the first time since drafting Gordon Hayward. It was once again back to the drawing board for the Utah Jazz.

Breaking Out

The 2013-14 offseason became a transition period for the Utah Jazz. They would lose their top frontcourt players, Paul Millsap and Al Jefferson, to free agency. Mo Williams also moved elsewhere, which meant that three of their starters had left the team. Despite that, they were still able to secure good talent from the draft. The Jazz drafted Trey Burke with their ninth overall draft pick, hoping that he would become the point guard of the future for them. They also found a gem in the young 7'1" Rudy Gobert from France with the 27th overall pick of the 2013 NBA Draft. The addition of veteran Richard Jefferson was also an important aspect of their offseason.

Gordon Hayward, who was the third leading scorer on the team last season, was the only productive player left in the lineup. Though he played mostly off the bench the past season, he was going to be their new go-to guy. This meant that he would have to carry the squad on his back as a 23-year-old looking to become the new leader of a young Utah Jazz team that was in the middle of a transition and rebuilding period.

Coming into the 2013-14 season, many suspected that Gordon Hayward would become the Utah Jazz's new point forward and playmaker. Trey Burke was still a rookie that could not yet run the Jazz offense on a full-time basis. There were also no other talented playmakers on the roster to fill in that gap. Because of that, Hayward was expected to play the role of a facilitator and floor general for the Jazz as a guard and forward hybrid in the upcoming season.

To be a point forward, as legendary head coach Don Nelson would say, a player must be 6'5" or taller, can be a good leader, productive rebounder, has a good assist to turnover ratio, and can defend multiple positions. Those were points that Gordon Hayward had to cover if he wanted to excel as the Utah Jazz's playmaker at guard/forward spot.[viii]

As a leader, Gordon Hayward was thrust into a position in an instant when Millsap and Jefferson left. He never had to be a leader during his first three seasons. However, considering that he was already the longest-tenured Jazz player despite being only 23 years old, Hayward was put into that spot without a choice but was willing to take the challenge of becoming the new face of the franchise. During training camp, he was often seen being more vocal than he ever was while his teammates were also seemingly responsive to his voice. This was a role that Hayward never had to assume since he was in his second season with Butler.[viii]

As for rebounding, Gordon Hayward was an influential player on the boards back in college and even in high school. However, that had yet to translate to the NBA. Playing with strong rebounders like Al Jefferson and Paul Millsap meant that Hayward never had to rebound the ball that much. Off the bench, he also had equally gifted rebounders in Derrick Favors and Enes Kanter. But without Jefferson and Millsap, much of the rebounding would have to fall on Favors and Kanter, who were going to be new to their starting spot. Hayward would have to play harder on the boards to help the pair of young big men flanking him.

As a defender, Gordon Hayward is not so bad either. He is one of the more underrated defenders at the small forward position. He does not wow anyone with his ability to play lockdown or with quick hands, but often plays that end of the floor smart enough to limit his mistakes. He is also not bad when factoring in his blocks per 36 minutes.

Gordon Hayward's assist to turnover ratio is something that needed improvement, though it was suspected that he would be a better playmaker in the upcoming season. Hayward was not used to being a consistent playmaker during his first three seasons, but had shown promise in that aspect of the game, especially when he ran pick-and-rolls with Paul Millsap back when the latter was still in Utah.

Making Gordon Hayward a point forward or playmaker was a beneficial move for the Utah Jazz because of their lack of production at the point guard spot. It could also help improve Hayward's abilities as a leader or even his stature as the Jazz's designated go-to guy on every play on the floor and not just in the scoring aspect of the game. The Jazz's lack of depth at the shooting guard spot and with Richard Jefferson slated to become a starter also meant that Hayward would play the two-guard position a lot of times. This meant that he would have to handle the ball and make plays more often than he was used to in the past seasons.

When the 2013-14 season started, Gordon Hayward played up to the expectations. In his second game of the season, he nearly had a triple-double after going for 18 points, ten rebounds, and eight assists against the Phoenix Suns. Then on November 5, 2014 he had 22 points, five rebounds, and four assists against the Brooklyn Nets. He immediately surpassed that mark a night later by going for 28 points, nine rebounds, and five assists versus the Boston Celtics. Immediately starting the season with four games of at least 20 points in just his first eight outings, Hayward had 24 and 22 points against the Raptors and Nuggets respectively.

Despite the fact that Gordon Hayward started the first eight games averaging 19.5 points, 6.1 rebounds, 4.4 assists, and 1.3 steals, the Jazz lost all of those outings to start the season 0-8. They would tally their first win on November 13 against the New Orleans Pelicans. Hayward had his second double-double that night and a career high in assists. He finished the game with 27 points, five rebounds, ten assists, and two steals. Against the same team one week later, he topped that assist mark by going for 11. However, the Jazz lost that one.

On November 25 in a win over the Chicago Bulls, Gordon Hayward would have a new career high in assists for the third time that season. He finished the game with 12 dimes in addition to 15 points and six rebounds. At that point, he was living up to the expectations of him being a steady facilitator and a secondary playmaker for the Utah Jazz, who were losing despite their franchise player's improved performances.

Against the Houston Rockets on December 2, Gordon Hayward had a new season high of 29 points. In that win, he relied more on his midrange game and his ability to get to the basket. He was 12 of 18 from the floor and did not attempt a single three-pointer. But that was not the best outing that Gordon Hayward had early in the season.

On December 13 against the Denver Nuggets, Gordon Hayward had what was arguably his best game as a pro at that point in his career. Scoring at least 30 points for the first time since he was a rookie, Hayward had 30 points on 11 out of 18 shooting from the floor. He also added a career-high mark of 13 rebounds and had five assists in that win for the Utah Jazz.

Hayward would have two more double-double outings as the year was ending. On December 21, he had 12 points and ten rebounds in a win against the Charlotte Bobcats. Two days later, he had a near triple-double of 16 points, 11 rebounds, and nine assists against the Memphis Grizzlies in a loss. And although he was an assist shy of a double-double four days later against the Lakers, he finished that win with 24 points, five rebounds, nine assists, and three steals.

Those who criticized Gordon Hayward for his lack of a killer instinct and mentality to dominate games would be shocked to see what he did on January 7, 2014. Just after back-to-back games of scoring 22 points to start the new year, Hayward took the challenge of matching up against eventual season MVP and four-time scoring champion Kevin Durant in that game against the OKC Thunder. In what was his new best game at that point in his career, Hayward converted 13 of his 16 shots and 9 of his 13 free throws to score a new career high of 37 points. He also added 11 rebounds and seven assists for a great all-around game. While Durant finished the game with 48 points, Hayward was the more efficient player that night. The Jazz also got the win from the Thunder.

After that game, Gordon Hayward would miss five straight outings with a left hip flexor. Despite the injury, Hayward said that he would play like he normally does when he gets back on the court. He was true to his word. In his return game on January 21, he had 27 points, five rebounds, five assists, and three steals in a loss to the Minnesota Timberwolves. He played like nothing was wrong with him and as if he was never out for two weeks.

Unfortunately for Hayward, he would see a slump in his shooting for about a month. He continued to play good all-around basketball by providing rebounds and assists for his team. However, he struggled with his shooting and would even score less than 10 points in seven of the next 13 games. In that span, he averaged only 11 points on a 31% shooting clip, though he was still productive on the rebounding and playmaking aspects of the game.

On February 26, Hayward would break out of the slump by going for another near triple-double effort. He went for 17 points, ten rebounds, and nine assists in that win against the Phoenix Suns. And four days later, he would go for at least 20 points for the first time in more than a month. He had 21 points in a loss to Indiana in front of his hometown crowd.

After playing the month of March on a steady basis, Gordon Hayward would go for at least 30 points for only the fourth time in his career. Against the Detroit Pistons on that March 24 night, he had 32 points on 10 out of 19 shooting from the floor. He would then finish the next 11 games scoring in double digits to cap off a 16-game scoring run of putting up at least 10 points. He ended the season short of another triple-double after going for 23 points, ten rebounds, and nine assists against the Minnesota Timberwolves in a win on April 16.

At season's end, Gordon Hayward averaged a team-high 16.2 points in addition to 5.1 rebounds and 5.2 assists. For the third straight season, he increased his scoring average while also improving on the other aspects of his game. However, his field goal shooting dropped to 41% as he adjusted to being the go-to guy of the team and as defenses continued to focus on him more. Unfortunately for him, the Jazz only won 25 games during the regular season. Despite the setbacks, the bright spot for the Jazz was that Gordon Hayward had already broken out and was on his way to eventually become a star in the NBA.

Hayward improved so well that season that he earned the praise of then-Memphis Grizzlies head coach Dave Joerger. He described Hayward as a terrific player that everybody should make their kids emulate. He played the game hard in all aspects while maintaining his stand as a player that could still improve. For a defensive specialist like Joerger, he even thought that the Jazz's franchise player was a tough cover because of his ability to shoot the ball at a high level.[iv]

But one matter that has to be seen from Gordon Hayward's 2013-14 season was that he was exposed on the offensive end. Most of his shots were coming from the perimeter where he was as deadly as any shooter can be. However, defenses started to close out on him well and took away his midrange jumpers. At that point in his career, he was yet to mature his slashing game, though his ball handles had improved to the point that he could already get to the basket. However, he just was not yet strong enough to finish in traffic and against contact. That was one of the few things that he worked on during the offseason.

But before Gordon Hayward had a chance to improve his game, he had to go through the rigors of free agency. As a restricted free agent during the 2014 offseason, Hayward was free to entertain suitors. The Charlotte Hornets tendered him a $63 million contract over the next three years. The Jazz did not offer him a larger and longer contract. Instead, they merely matched the offer by the Hornets to keep Hayward for the next three years. As time would tell, this would later come back to bite them.

After he was signed to a three-year extension, Gordon Hayward was selected as a member of the 2014 Team USA Select Team to determine a 12-man roster for the FIBA World Championships. He did pretty well as a finalist but could not break into the roster because the team went to opposite extremes by going for guards and big men. Nevertheless, Hayward loved the experience because of how detail-oriented the coaching staff was. It was a chance for him to learn under some of the best coaches and with some of the best players in the NBA.[iv]

Gordon Hayward was already at one of the highest points in his life at that time after getting married, earning a large and lucrative contract, seeing his name as a finalist of Team USA, and making leaps and bounds as a franchise player. But he still believed that he had more things to do to improve on his game. In his own words, he still had more room to grow and a lot more places to go.[iv]

It was during the offseason when Gordon Hayward filled in that room he had to grow into. The Butler product that used to look like a college poster boy with his mopped hair and his skinny frame would transform almost overnight. Hayward would ditch that mop-top hairdo and sported a fresh-cut brushed-up look that made him look so clean. And from that boyish clean look, Hayward would grow his facial hair to look more rugged than he ever was.

To complement his new manly look, Gordon Hayward would also transform his body. He would spend the offseason in the weight room and improved his diet to bulk his body up. His muscles began to look larger, toned, and more defined than they ever were. Gone was the skinny boyish Gordon Hayward that seemed fit for a boy band. Instead, here was a Gordon Hayward that looked like he was going to steal your girlfriend by force. He would even describe himself as a "bully," which is a term that never fit him before.[ix]

With his improved body frame, Gordon Hayward said that he felt a lot stronger than he ever did in his life. Using his strength, Hayward stated that he could already bully defenders in practice for the first time in his life. During training camp, he had increased his weight to 230 pounds, which was ten more pounds than the previous season. However, Hayward said that he planned on trimming down to 225 to regain the speed and mobility he lost from the added muscle.[ix]

Knowing that the NBA is more about speed than strength or muscle, Gordon Hayward would also work on his mobility and speed to counteract the amount of mass he gained during the offseason. With his added strength coupled with his speed retention, Hayward was expected to be more efficient with his shot the upcoming season because he could take the ball to the basket and bang bodies with defenders.

The Jazz's new head coach Quin Snyder was also impressed by how much Gordon Hayward seemed to improve from the previous season. He was the standout performer during Utah's training camp, and as teammate Alec Burks would say, he had become more of a complete leader at the age of 24. But leadership was not the only thing that Snyder expected of him. The new head coach wanted Hayward to become aggressive, which was what he was often criticized for lacking in most of his pre-draft scouting reports. For Snyder, he believed that the only way that Hayward could be more efficient was for him to be aggressive.[ix] And because of the way he improved his body, the former Bulldog would now be able to take his aggression to the next level.

As the 2014-15 season was approaching, Gordon Hayward was vocal about how he felt he had already become one of the best players in the league. With the new offensive system that Snyder implemented, he would still be a playmaker, but not as much as he was under Corbin. However, Hayward believed that he would thrive more as a scorer because of the spacing and ball movement the Utah Jazz wanted to implement in the upcoming season. With that, Hayward added a new goal to his childhood list. He wanted to be an All-Star.[ix]

But for him to be an All-Star, Gordon Hayward knew that the best way to do so was to help his team succeed. Not a lot could be said about the Jazz's 25-win season the past year. While they were surely going to improve, nobody knew what to expect from them. That was where Hayward was needed. He already had the talent, maturity, and improved leadership. The only thing he needed to do was to carry his team to playoff contention.

Gordon Hayward would start his first two games of the 2014-15 season slow. He would combine for only 24 points on a 7 out of 20 shooting clip in losses to the Houston Rockets and the Dallas Mavericks. However, in Utah's first win that season, he starred. Hayward led a blowout against the Phoenix Suns by going for 24 points and ten rebounds. Everything fell into place soon after.

Though it came at a loss to the LA Clippers, Hayward would have 27 points, seven rebounds, and five assists on November 3. He shot 10 out of 19 from the field while also making 5 of his 12 attempts from the three-point line. Hayward followed that up with a win against Cleveland. Matching up against a returning LeBron James, he put up 21 points and seven assists to give his team that win. His step back jumper near the end of the game was what sealed the victory for Utah. What was also clear that night was that not even LeBron James could outmuscle and bully the much-improved Gordon Hayward.

In a loss to the Indiana Pacers on November 10, Hayward played well in front of his hometown crowd. He put up 30 points on an 11 for 15 shooting night. Four days later, he topped that performance in a win over the New York Knicks. Gordon Hayward had 33 points on an 11 out of 18 shooting performance. Then, a little over a week later, he would showcase his newfound aggression by living at the free throw line in a loss to the New Orleans Pelicans. He was 9 out of 16 from the floor and 11 out of 14 from the foul stripe to score 31 points in addition to eight rebounds. Hayward would then score at least 30 points for the fourth time when he had 30 against the Clippers on November 29 in a loss.

As defenses locked down on him and as the Utah Jazz stumbled a few games, Hayward bounced back in a win over the Miami Heat on December 17. He shot an efficient 9 out of 13 from the floor to score 29 points. He also had six rebounds and seven assists that night. He would then end a fruitful 2014 by going for 26 points in a win against the Timberwolves on December 30.

At that point, Gordon Hayward had already begun to make doubters eat their words. There were a lot of critics that believed he was never worth a max contract. Some Jazz fans were even ready to move on from him when the Hornets offered him a three-year max contract the past offseason. Of course, it was normal to think that way. After all, Hayward only averaged 16 points on a dismal 40% shooting clip the past season. However, the Utah Jazz knew how hard of a worker he was and how far he could go as a franchise player.[x]

Gordon Hayward seemed like a whole new player that season. He was sinking shots and making layups that he could not before. Some would credit his added strength for that. After all, he had been seen converting shots even when defenders got physical with him. However, his balance could also be a factor in his improved play. Gordon Hayward was one of the best players at converting shots with defenders within two to four feet of him. He was even better than proven scorers DeMar DeRozan and Carmelo Anthony at that, though he did not take as many tight shots as they did. This only goes to show how of smart a shot-taker Hayward was.[x] The Butler product was finally proving himself as a rising star in the NBA.

One of Gordon Hayward's best games early in January of 2015 was when he had 31 points on 12 out of 18 shooting from the floor and 4 out of 7 shooting from the three-point line against the LA Lakers on January 16. Six days later, he would go for 24 points, six rebounds, and six assists in a win against the

Milwaukee Bucks before torching the Brooklyn Nets in a blowout win with 24 points on a 71% shooting clip. In the final game of the month, he had a fantastic game against a dominant Golden State Warriors team in a win for the Jazz. He had 26 points, 15 rebounds, six assists, and three steals.

By February, it seemed as if he was lobbying coaches to put him in the All-Star Game. He had back-to-back high-scoring outputs against the Sacramento Kings and the New Orleans Pelicans in wins for the Jazz. He had 30 points on 13 out of 23 shooting in that game against the Kings. He then went for 32 points, seven rebounds, eight assists, and two steals against the Pelicans. Unfortunately, Hayward was not selected as an All-Star not because of his play, but because the Jazz were still far from being playoff contenders.

Despite not making the All-Star team, Hayward continued his consistency. He scored in double digits in all but two of his final 23 games to end the season.

He had 12 games of scoring at least 20 points during that span. He would average a new career-best 19.3 points while also adding 4.9 rebounds and 4.1 assists during the season. Hayward also improved his shooting to nearly 45%. His three-point accuracy was also markedly improved at 36%. The 38-win Utah Jazz would fail to make the postseason despite the improvements.

Despite not making the postseason, the Utah Jazz had plenty of things to be happy about. They had improved remarkably from the Ty Corbin era. From being a team that relied more on offense, Snyder made the Jazz a slower paced team that won games on the defensive end. They were one of the lowest scoring teams in the league but were the best at limiting their opponents' points. Hayward's improvement also was not the only good news they had. Derrick Favors emerged as a significant inside presence. Meanwhile, late first round pick Rudy Gobert showed signs of promise as a paint defender and as a terrific rebounder. He made Enes

Kanter dispensable. Because of the Jazz's improved frontline, Gordon Hayward was allowed more freedom to operate, not only on the offensive end, but on the defensive side of things as well.

As Gordon Hayward prepared for the 2015 offseason, it had already become apparent that he was the answer to the Utah Jazz's question of who would emerge as their new star after trading away Deron Williams back in 2011. It was not long ago when Jazz fans booed when Hayward was selected ninth overall during the 2010 NBA Draft. It was not also long ago when he was a young man getting scolded by teammates for mental lapses and getting bullied by stronger players.

The skills were always there for Gordon Hayward. He was always a good shooter, respectable ball handler, smart defender, and deceptive athletic finisher. While most people would say that all it took for him was to grow into his body and add muscle to his frame, it was evident that everything wrong with Hayward back then was in the mental aspect. He was young, inexperienced, and too shy to take over games. As he would say, things were different back then. Gordon Hayward was now more mature.[xi]

Long ago, not many could imagine that Gordon Hayward was going to be a player good enough to become a borderline All-Star. Not a lot saw his potential, if he did have any. He was all hard work and humility. He kept himself quiet on his way to becoming the Utah Jazz's newest franchise player. Gordon Hayward would take his versatility to the next level and become one of the best small forwards while markedly and gradually improving his game every offseason. Not a lot of players get better every year. There are some that would show up one season but would suddenly regress in the years to come. But Hayward consistently brought something new to the table every season while also carrying with him a Utah Jazz team looking to get back to the playoffs.

From being regarded solely as a shooter, whose ceiling was a glorified role player, Gordon Hayward transformed himself into a utility star for the Utah Jazz. He did everything for them. Outside of the center position, he played every possible role there is for the Jazz. He was their top scorer and go-to guy on the offensive end. He has often played the power forward role in small lineups. He played the role of a spot-up shooter. He made up for Utah's lack of elite playmaking at the point guard spot. He would even lock up the opposing team's best players from time to time. At that point, it was already safe to say that Hayward had become one of the best players in the entire NBA.

Coming into the 2015-16 season, Gordon Hayward sported the same supporting cast that has helped him turn the Utah Jazz into a scary defensive squad. Flanked by the two terrifying paint presences in Rudy Gobert and Derrick Favors, and joined by the much-improved wing scorer Rodney Hood, Hayward was on his way to another productive season of improvements, not only to himself, but also to the Jazz.

Hayward would start the season slowly, barely making anything from the field in his first four games. The first time he would break the 20-point barrier that season was on November 5, 2015, in a win over the Denver Nuggets. Gordon Hayward had 20 points on 7 out of 13 shooting that game. A week after that, he had his first 20-10 double-double performance of the season. In that narrow loss to the Miami Heat, Hayward had 24 points and 11 rebounds.

On November 25, Gordon Hayward would have his then-season high of 33 points in a win against the Los Angeles Clippers. He made half of his 22 shots and 5 of his seven three-point attempts in that outing. That was when Hayward would start to perform on a more consistent basis as the season went on. He would score at least 20 points five times over the course of the next eight games for the Utah Jazz. And before the year

2015 ended, he had his second double-double of 23 points and ten rebounds on December 31 in a win against the Portland Trailblazers.

On January 9, 2016, Gordon Hayward would top his previous season high by going for 34 points in a win over the Miami Heat. He made 14 of his 22 shots from the floor in that game. He would have gotten more points had he performed up to his standards from the foul line. Gordon Hayward was a mere 4 out of 10 from the free throw line in that game. It was uncharacteristic of a player that has made over 80% of his foul shots in the last four seasons. Nevertheless, a win was a win with him scoring 34 points.

Gordon Hayward would top that season high on January 18 in an overtime loss to the Charlotte Hornets, the team that he intended to join had the Jazz not matched his contract nearly two years ago. In that game, he had 36 points, five rebounds, nine assists, and two steals. He made half of his 24 shots and also half of his 12 three-pointers in that outing. Just two days after that, he would make all 10 of his free throws in a narrow loss to the Knicks. He had 27 points in that game.

On February 1, Gordon Hayward nearly had a triple-double in what was one of his best all-around efforts that season. In that win versus the Chicago Bulls, the Butler product had 27 points, 12 rebounds, and seven assists in nearly 44 minutes of play for the Utah Jazz. That was the third game of what was going to be a seven-game win streak for the Jazz. Gordon Hayward averaged 20 points, six rebounds, and four assists during that winning run. In that final game of that streak, Hayward capped off a win against the Dallas Mavericks with a step back game-winner that broke the hearts of the Mavs' fans.

When the All-Star Weekend came rolling, Gordon Hayward was yet again a snub despite showing more consistency and improvement to his game that season.

It was hard to imagine who Hayward could have replaced in that Western Conference All-Star team considering that everyone on that squad deserved the spot. Despite the snub, it did not take away the fact that Gordon Hayward was a star still on the rise. He was averaging stellar numbers of 20.6 points, 4.8 rebounds, and four assists during February. He never scored under 10 points the entire month, and it was becoming clear how consistent of a scorer he had become.

In his first game of March, Hayward would go for 26 points and six assists in a loss to the Toronto Raptors. Just three days later on March 5, he would go for 24 points, five rebounds, and four assists in a win against the New Orleans Pelicans. Hayward's high for that month was on March 13 in a win against the Sacramento Kings. He posted 27 points on a 9 out of 19 shooting clip in that game. That was also his highest scoring output from then on until the end of the season, though he would have a double-double outing of 24 points and 13 rebounds later on in a loss to the Clippers on April 8.

The final highlight of Gordon Hayward's season was that he was there on the court facing Kobe Bryant in the Black Mamba's last NBA game before retiring. With playoff contention well behind them as the Houston Rockets managed to secure the final seed even if the Jazz were to win that game against the Lakers, the Jazz went out there with nothing to lose and nothing to gain.

Gordon Hayward was one of the few players to guard Kobe that night. Five years ago, he was a mere rookie that outplayed Bryant and defended him well. This time, however, Kobe Bryant wanted to exit the league in style. Against one of the toughest defenses in the league, Bryant won the game for the Lakers by dropping 60 points in his final performance. After that performance by Bryant, the only thing that Gordon Hayward could say was that the entire Jazz team was shocked by how aggressive the legendary player was in his final NBA game. Fortunately for Hayward, that would not be the last time he would see Kobe on a basketball court.

At the end of the 2015-16 regular season, Gordon Hayward once more improved his scoring numbers. He would average 19.7 points, five rebounds, and 3.7 assists. However, the Jazz would once again fail to make the postseason with a 40-42 win-loss record. Despite that, they were still one of the best defensive teams in the league, though their scoring was only ranked number 28 in the entire NBA. They were the slowest pace in the entire league and had found their calling as a defensive squad under Quin Snyder.

Despite another improved season for him and the Jazz, Gordon Hayward could not help but feel disappointed. He had only made the playoffs once in the six years he had spent in the NBA, and that trip ended with a sweep. Not only was he looking to make the postseason once more, but he was also wishing he could taste what it was like to win in the playoffs.

Nevertheless, Gordon Hayward was still the proud leader that gave his team the credit for putting up a fight the entire season. Though he felt that the Jazz should have been in the playoffs, he was proud of the way his team battled against adversity game after game. He was more than happy with the way he and his teammates gave the team a shot at a playoff spot despite their youth and inexperience.[iv] But that was the last time he would be happy about being on the outside looking in. The next time he would watch a playoff game, it was not from the comforts of his own home. He wanted to be in it with his teammates.

All-Star Status, Final Season in Utah

Gordon Hayward immediately went back to work as soon as the offseason started. Instead of going home to Indiana, he opted to stay in Utah to work with the coaching staff. He even skipped the chance to play for

Team USA in the 2016 Olympics because of how much he wanted to spend time with his family and on his craft the entire offseason. He challenged himself the whole summer, hoping that he still had plenty of room to grow into a player that could lead his team to the playoffs.

One of the few things that Gordon Hayward worked on during the summer was his midrange game, and who better to help him with it than Kobe Bryant himself. Hayward was all but helpless when Bryant was dropping 60 points on his team in the final game of the regular season on April 13, 2016. He has also spent his childhood and teen days watching Kobe draining midrange jumpers over defenders in a career that spanned two decades. Probably no other player in league history was better at creating a space to pull up for a midrange jumper than Kobe Bryant was. Hayward knew this and had to seek the help of the expert himself.

Gordon Hayward started off by running through sets without a ball. He then spent time watching film on Kobe Bryant's workout and techniques. It then hit him that he had to do something out of the ordinary to be able to take his game to the next level. He would reach out to Kobe and ask if the retired superstar was willing to help him with his game. Fortunately, Bryant agreed.[xii]

Gordon Hayward would spend an entire week with Kobe Bryant in Newport Beach in California. He soaked up some of Bryant's teachings regarding the art of the midrange game. Bryant himself learned from Jordan. He then perfected his craft from there. Hayward, who thought that it was one of the most productive weeks of his life, would go on to learn from one of the greatest to ever lace them up.[xii] All he had left to do was to perfect his craft and make the midrange game a weapon as deadly as Bryant's was in the 20 years that the Mamba has played in the NBA.

Fortunately for Gordon Hayward, he was not the only one looking to improve. The entire Utah Jazz team improved its roster. While the core of Hayward, Gobert, and Favors was intact, they would add multiple-time All-Star and veteran scorer Joe Johnson. While Johnson was no longer the primetime player he used to be, he was still known as a big shot-maker and a leadership presence on the floor. And making up for the lack of production at the point guard spot, they signed George Hill during the offseason. Hill's backcourt defense and ability to run the offense and shoot the jumper would be a valuable addition to the Jazz.

Gordon Hayward would, however, face a minor setback before the season started. He would fracture a finger in his left hand before the 2016-17 season even got started. All that hard work during the offseason bit him in a minor way, though, and he would miss the first six games of the season because of that injury.

The Jazz held strong by winning half of those games even without their best player.

The moment Gordon Hayward returned to the lineup and made his season debut, it was clear that he meant business. Hayward would have 28 points on 6 out of 17 shooting from the floor and a perfect 14 for 14 from the free throw line to help give his team a win against the New York Knicks on November 6. A night later, he then led the Jazz to a blowout win against the Philadelphia 76ers by going for 20 points in only 30 minutes of play. He then had 29 points the next game, though it was a loss to the Charlotte Hornets. Nevertheless, he made up for it by going for 20 points, ten rebounds, and eight assists in a win against the Orlando Magic before hitting the Miami Heat with 25 points, nine rebounds, and four assists.

In an instant after getting Gordon Hayward back, the Utah Jazz seemed like they were on the cusp of becoming contenders. They had won four of the last five games since Hayward's return. Hayward himself had the best five-game start he had ever had in his career. He scored at least 20 points in all five of those games and averaged 24.4 points, 7.6 rebounds, and 4.2 assists along the way. It was clear that he was out for blood that season.

While the Utah Jazz would slow down after seeing a four-game losing skid, Hayward would power them back by leading the team to win seven of their next eight games. It was arguably Hayward's best eight-game stretch. He started by going for 22 points against the Nuggets in a blowout win. He then had two 24-point games after that before exploding for 31 points against the Houston Rockets on November 29. In that lone loss during that eight-game run, he had 32 points on a 12 out of 22 shooting performance in a one-point loss to the Miami Heat on December 1. He then had 32 again against Denver before going for 23 and 28 against the Lakers and the Suns respectively after that.

Proving that his game had matured and that his midrange jumper had become as deadly of a weapon as any other in the entire league, Gordon Hayward averaged 27 points, 5.1 rebounds, and four assists during that run. He even shot nearly 50% from the floor and exactly 50% from the three-point line in those eight games. While Gordon Hayward was not expected to maintain such performances the entire season, it was evident how much better he has gotten over the offseason.

The next time Gordon Hayward would crack the 30-point mark was on December 27 against the Los Angeles Lakers. In that win for the Utah Jazz, Hayward made 10 of his 17 shots to score 31 points while also grabbing nine rebounds in the process. That was the first of what was going to be a four-game win for the Jazz. He ended that mini-streak with 30 points against the Brooklyn Nets on January 2, 2017.

While Gordon Hayward would not score over 30 points again the entire month of January, he did well enough to be a consistent scoring threat for Utah. The Jazz would also perform surprisingly well during that month having lost only six of the 15 games they played in January. In those 15 games, Hayward averaged 21 points and 4.7 rebounds. He shot 46.6% from the field during January. It was also during that month when Gordon Hayward was named to the Western All-Stars as a reserve.

Starting All-Star month on a good note, Gordon Hayward had 27 points on 8 out of 13 shooting from the floor against the Milwaukee Bucks in a win on February 1. He followed that up with 33 points on 13 out of 20 shooting against the Hornets in another win. Rounding up that fantastic three-game run to start February, he had 30 points, seven rebounds, and five assists in a blowout win against the Atlanta Hawks on February 6.

On February 9, Gordon Hayward would score a then-season high 36 points in a loss to the Dallas Mavericks. He hit 13 of his 27 shots that night. He followed that performance up with 31 points on 10 out of 19 shooting from the floor against the Boston Celtics just two nights later. However, that too turned out to be a loss for the Utah Jazz.

Gordon Hayward would finally make his much-awaited All-Star Game debut on February 19, 2017, in New Orleans, Louisiana. With that All-Star berth, Hayward became only one of 12 Jazz players to make the team. The last Jazz player to do it was Deron Williams in 2011. He was only the third person to make the All-Star team as a member of the Utah Jazz in the last ten years. During that span, only Deron Williams and Carlos Boozer were able to make the cut as Jazz players. He was also one of four first-time All-Stars in that event. Hayward would score 8 points in 17 minutes during the midseason classic to help the West win the game.

In his first game back from the All-Star Game, Gordon Hayward would go for 29 points on an efficient 11 out of 17 clip from the field in that win over the Milwaukee Bucks. Two days later on February 26, he would light the Washington Wizards up with 30 points and nine rebounds. It was another win for the Utah Jazz, who were seemingly peaking at the right time that season. Having one of his best months that season, Hayward averaged 25.5 points and five rebounds during February. He shot 51% from the floor and 40% from the three-point area that month.

After consistent performances for a competitive Utah Jazz team, Gordon Hayward would go for a new career high that season. In a loss to the Pacers in front of his hometown crowd, Hayward would go for 38 points on 16 out of 24 shooting from the field. But that was not his best performance that season. He would record another career high on April 7 just a game after scoring 30 on the Portland Trailblazers. In that new career game, Gordon Hayward would go for 14 out of

22 from the field, 4 out of 5 from the three-point area, and 7 out of 8 from the foul line to score 39 points.

As the dust settled, Gordon Hayward averaged 21.9 points, 5.4 rebounds, and 3.5 assists during his first All-Star season. Once again, he increased his scoring averages while also collecting career highs in rebounds that season. He would also shoot 47% from the floor, which was his best shooting clip excluding his rookie season. Hayward also shot nearly 40% from the three-point area that season.

More importantly, the Utah Jazz made the playoffs as the fifth seed by winning 51 games during the season. While some would credit the Utah Jazz's much improved slow-paced style of defense, which ranked third overall for efficiency in the entire league thanks to the efforts of the improved Rudy Gobert, it was Gordon Hayward's improved scoring and leadership that lifted them up. When the Jazz were unable to get wing production from the often injured Alec Burks and

Rodney Hood that season, Hayward gave them a spark as the lone scoring option from the perimeter. But Hayward's mission was not yet over. He still had to lead his team during the playoffs, hoping that he could get deeper than he did when he first made it there several years ago.

In the first round of the playoffs, the Utah Jazz would go up against the Los Angeles Clippers, a team they tied in wins during the regular season. It was regarded as the most exciting playoff series in the West during the first round. The Utah Jazz drew first blood in Game 1. Hayward led the way in that playoff game with 19 points and ten rebounds proving that he was also a primetime performer in the postseason. While Hayward was the leader of the Jazz, it was a buzzer-beating layup from veteran closer Joe Johnson that sealed the win for Utah.

Gordon Hayward would also play well in Game 2, though the Clippers would take that one. Coming home to Utah after stealing home court advantage, Gordon Hayward was on fire in Game 3. He was shooting the lights out from everywhere. He shot 13 out of 21 from the floor, 4 out of 8 from the three-point area, and 10 out of 11 from the foul line. He would eventually end up with a career-high 40 points together with ten rebounds and four assists. Unfortunately, the Clippers got back their home court advantage by winning Game 3.

Game 4 was an unfortunate one for Gordon Hayward. Playing only 9 minutes the entire game and scoring only 3 points, it was evident that he was not himself. The Jazz would take him out of the match because he was suffering from food poisoning. Despite his absence, the Jazz saw a resurgent performance from backup wingmen Joe Johnson and Rodney Hood. The veteran former All-Star had 28 points while the improved Hood had 18 markers.

Returning to the lineup for Game 5, Gordon Hayward led the way for his team to regain the series lead. He made 9 of his 16 shots and half of his eight three-pointers to score 27 points while also grabbing eight rebounds and dishing out four assists in the process. And though he had 31 in Game 6, the Clippers would nonetheless manage to force Game 7.

Playing Game 7 in LA in front of a hostile crowd, Gordon Hayward put the team on his back. While the Jazz focused on defense, it was Hayward's offense that gave them the firepower needed to win the game and proceed to the next round. The All-Star wing would go for 26 points, eight rebounds, and three assists to give his team a 13-point win and to proceed to the second round for the first time in his career. In that hard-fought seven-game series, Hayward averaged 23.7 points and 7.3 rebounds. The only blemish was that Game 4 he had to exit due to food poisoning. He performed extremely well in that series.

Unfortunately, the playoffs got a lot tougher. In the second round, the Jazz had to face the league-leading Golden State Warriors, who seemed unbeatable with MVP's Kevin Durant and Stephen Curry leading a team of four All-Stars. It was a single All-Star in Gordon Hayward against what is regarded as one of the best, if not the best, teams in the history of the entire NBA.

In Game 1, Gordon Hayward could not catch the same fire he had the whole series against the Clippers. He shot only 4 out of 15 from the floor and was limited to merely 12 points. He would bounce back in Game 2 by going for 33 points on 11 out of 21 shooting against a collection of good defenders like Kevin Durant and Andre Iguodala. He performed just as admirably in Game 3. By constantly attacking the basket and getting fouled, he made 13 of his 14 shots to add up to the 29 points he had. Then in Game 4, he would go for 25 points. Unfortunately for the Jazz, the Warriors won all four of those games by double digits. Utah was severely outmatched in that sweep.

Despite losing via a sweep in the playoffs for the second time in his career, Gordon Hayward proved that he was not merely a regular season performer. In the 11 games he played during the postseason, he averaged 24.1 points, 6.1 rebounds, and 3.4 assists. He shot 44% from the floor overall and over 40% from the three-point line the entire playoffs. However, it seemed like that Game 4 blowout loss to the Warriors was Gordon Hayward's final game for the Jazz.

The Move to Boston

When the season ended, Gordon Hayward's three-year contract with the Utah Jazz also ended. He was an unrestricted free agent during the offseason. Had the Jazz decided to not just match the Hornets' offer back in 2014 and had they tendered their long-term extension to Hayward, they would have had him for a longer time and would have seen more All-Star production from him. However, they handled that 2014 contract negotiation as badly as they could. Hayward's 2017 free agency would bite them.

As a free agent, Gordon Hayward was able to sign with any team that offered him a contract while the Jazz were not even allowed to match it. Considered one of the best small forwards in the league and an All-Star still in the prime of his career, Gordon Hayward was one of the biggest names of the 2017 free agency period. With his versatile offense, all-around skills, and ability to play in any system, he was a sought-after commodity.

Gordon Hayward would shorten the list of his suitors to three teams. The first was the Miami Heat. The Boston Celtics, led by his former Butler coach Brad Stevens, was also one of his top choices. Of course returning to the Utah Jazz, the team that believed in him and was patient with him for seven seasons, was also an option he had on the back of his mind.

Hayward would go on to meet with Pat Riley and the Miami Heat. After the Heat pitched him a championship culture in Miami, Hayward was nearly convinced that he wanted to be a Heat. He felt how much he wanted to be a Heat and how the organization would make him feel at home. He even told his wife that he thought Miami was finally his NBA home. His wife agreed with him by saying that she could see herself living in Florida.[xiii]

Miami also had a collection of real talent and a championship caliber coach in Erik Spoelstra. The Heat boasted Hassan Whiteside, who had the same defensive capabilities as Utah's Rudy Gobert. They also had complete players in all positions. However, the small forward spot remained their hole. They were hoping Gordon Hayward would fill that gap. The star forward would not give a final word after the meeting, though he felt happy about the pitch that the Heat gave him.

Gordon Hayward would also note that the meeting he had with the Utah Jazz was just as excellent. In that meeting they had in Hayward's vacation home in San Diego, the Jazz pitched in several reasons to try to convince their star to stay in Utah. The Jazz were hoping they could keep the momentum running with Hayward leading them after winning 51 games the previous season. They also sold on him the prospect of being able to finish an entire career in Utah to become one of the best players they ever had, much like how John Stockton did. To convince the star, they even signed talented passer Ricky Rubio and re-inked Hayward's best friend Joe Ingles to a long-term deal.[xiv] Hoping they could also sign him to a long-term deal, the Jazz could offer as much as $172 million over the next five years for Hayward to stay. Other teams could only offer $128 million worth in four years. This left Hayward undecided just when he was about to imagine himself wearing a Miami Heat uniform.

Then Gordon Hayward met with the Boston Celtics. The Celtics are considered one of the most storied franchises in the entire NBA. Hall of Famers such as Larry Bird, Bill Russell, Bob Cousy, John Havlicek, and Kevin McHale, among others, have won titles and MVPs with the Celtics. It was the kind of legacy that would challenge Hayward to perform better and try to match his name up with those legendary players. The Celtics were also the top-seeded team in the Eastern Conference a year ago and were only going to get better.

The Boston Celtics boasted a young roster with plenty of fresh talent. At that time, they had high-scoring point guard Isaiah Thomas flanked by wingmen Jae Crowder, Jaylen Brown, and rookie acquisition Jayson Tatum. The paint was anchored by former All-Star Al Horford while Marcus Smart was a productive player off the bench. Just looking at the roster, which was built to win, was enough for Gordon Hayward to move to Boston. However, there was one more factor.

Back in 2014 when Brad Stevens had just finished his first year in the NBA as the new head coach of the Boston Celtics, he texted then restricted free agent Gordon Hayward. He told his former Butler player how much he longed to reunite with him once more though he was already aware that the Celtics were in no position to sign him at that time. Fast forward three seasons ago, and Stevens had become one of the best coaches in the entire league. Like Hayward, who continued to improve every season since getting drafted in 2010, Stevens improved the Celtics every season from the time he took the job in 2013. The stars all seemed aligned for a reunion to happen. The former Butler head coach would then send a text to the former Butler player telling him that they were hoping to meet again. Brad Stevens, the man that gave him a scholarship several years ago believing he could one day become an NBA player, was a major factor in Gordon Hayward's decision.

The decision process was a family thing for Gordon Hayward. He had his father helping him make a decision. A fan-made video convincing the younger Gordon to stay in Utah left Gordon Sr. in tears and was almost sure to tell his son to stay with the Jazz. The elder Hayward also could not bear to see the backlash his son would get if he had joined a ready-made Celtics team. But after seeing the Cavs trashing Boston in the Eastern Conference Finals, he realized that the Celtics needed his son.

For Gordon Hayward, it was comforting for him to see familiar faces on the Celtics' staff greeting him and making him feel at home when they met. While he and Stevens remained close, the meeting they had with Celtics president Danny Ainge was productive as far as basketball would go. They told the All-Star how much they were envisioning him to become the versatile do-it-all wing player they needed to take the team to the next level. He was comfortable with the idea of playing under Stevens again and joining a talented team that could take the league by storm at any minute.

On July 4, 2017, Gordon Hayward would make his announcement and explain his decision on a piece on *The Player's Tribune*. He would thank the Utah Jazz for believing in him and for waiting patiently for him since 2010. However, Hayward had to make a choice. That choice was the Boston Celtics because he felt like he could win a championship there and he felt like he needed to leave his comfort zone. In Boston, he also had Brad Stevens, the only coach he has been able to talk to comfortably and count on when he needed someone to listen to him.[xv]

With that decision, his days as a Utah Jazz player were over. He would leave Utah with 8,077 career points scored with the team and a legacy as a player that worked hard every single season to reach stardom. He was Utah's best player in the post-Deron Williams era and was the epitome of what the people in Salt Lake

City were—hard-working. If there was a legacy he had left in Utah, it was not the lone All-Star appearance he had with the Jazz or the two playoff seasons they had. It was his patience, humility, and hard work that defined his legacy as a Jazz player. But now, he was on his way to taking those qualities with him elsewhere. He was bound for Boston.

Seven seasons ago, Gordon Hayward and Brad Stevens were on a miracle 25-game win streak heading into the 2010 NCAA Finals. Back then, Hayward was merely a 20-year-old skinny kid that has not yet grown into his body and his skill level. Stevens was the leader that would have the Butler Bulldogs give a tough fight to the Duke Blue Devils in the final game of March Madness. They were one shot away from winning the title. Unfortunately, Hayward missed his chance at a national championship with Brad Stevens.

After inking a four-year, $128 million contract with the Boston Celtics, Gordon Hayward now had an opportunity to finish something he started with Stevens. He could finally team up again with his college head coach in the hopes of winning a title together. They were in a great position to do so as Hayward's move to Boston made the Celtics one of the top contenders in the East.

Gordon Hayward was set to join a team with a logjam at the wing position. Boston had just recently drafted Jayson Tatum as a security blanket in case they could not sign Hayward. The young Jaylen Brown was also waiting in the wings to finally breakout as a young athletic player. While they previously had Jae Crowder, Boston decided to trade him along with Isaiah Thomas to acquire the Cleveland Cavalier's star point guard Kyrie Irving.

With Irving in the mix, Hayward would not be asked to carry the offensive load on his shoulders as much as he did in Utah. He also had capable defenders in Marcus Smart and Jaylen Brown to help him man the wings. Meanwhile, Al Horford was more than ready to help him out by defending the paint as the final line of defense for the Celtics. With all those pieces in place, Gordon Hayward would not have to shoulder the same amount of weight as he did as a Jazz player. Instead, he could focus on the things he needed to do. He was, of course, a scorer that the Celtics could look to off the catch and in broken play situations. And because Kyrie Irving is more of a scorer than a playmaker, Hayward would be able to man the point forward position more than he did back in Utah.

Not being asked to carry the offense on a full-time basis, Hayward would have more freedom off the ball in Brad Stevens' system of crisp ball movement. Considering that he has enough talent to be able to play off the ball as a shooter and cutter, Gordon Hayward was a perfect fit for the Celtics. And with him being asked to be a secondary scorer and a primary leader and utility guy for a talented Boston Celtics team, Gordon Hayward's ceiling for the upcoming 2017-18 season was a title or at least an appearance in the NBA Finals.

Chapter 5: Personal Life

Gordon Hayward Jr. is the son of Gordon Hayward Sr. and Jodi Hayward. He was born as the twin brother of Heather Hayward, a tennis player who starred in Butler and was a regular all-conference team member when she was at Brownsburg High School. Butler and was a consistent all-conference team member when she was in Brownsburg High School. Just like his sister, Gordon used to be a tennis player in high school but would devote his college athletic life to basketball.

Hayward married Robyn Van Vilet back in 2014. Both Gordon Hayward and Robyn Van Vilet went to high school in Indiana, though the latter finished her studies much later than the former did. They started dating in 2013 when Van Vilet was working as a beautician. Five months later, the couple got engaged and were married during the offseason of 2014.

The couple of Gordon Hayward and Robyn Van Vilet have two daughters together. The first one, Bernadette

Marie, was born on June 6, 2015. They would have their second child on July 11, 2016, when Charlotte Margaret was born. Their second daughter's birth was a primary reason for Hayward to skip on the 2016 Team USA training because he wanted to juggle time between being a father and a basketball player.

Other than basketball, Gordon Hayward spends time in other endeavors. One of his favorite past time is video gaming. He is an avid fan of video game franchises such as Halo, Starcraft, League of Legends, Defense of the Ancients, and classics such as Contra and Double Dragon, among others. He even took time to defend his love for video games on *The Players' Tribune*.[xvi] But since getting married, he visibly cut down on his video gaming to focus on being a family man and as a star player.

Back in college, Gordon Hayward also recorded a rap song entitled "Too Big, Yo." The song would not have the best critic reactions but would nonetheless be one of the theme songs of the Butler Bulldogs back when they made that miracle run to the NCAA title game back in 2010. Hayward has not recorded another track since.

Chapter 6: Impact on Basketball

Considering he has only started to play an All-Star brand of basketball just recently, Gordon Hayward is a player whose impact on the game of basketball is not yet on par with other elite small forward such as LeBron James, Kevin Durant, or Kawhi Leonard. However, his impact can be measured by how he developed from being a skinny player, whose ceiling was a rotation guy at best, to become one of the best perimeter players in the entire NBA.

From his days in high school where he was often overlooked because was not as strong and athletic or aggressive as some other players were, Gordon Hayward was a point guard converted into a small forward thanks largely to his sudden growth spurt. This kid was a tennis player who nearly quit basketball because he lacked the size to even get a Division I scholarship in college.

However, with enough hard work and determination (along with his growth spurt), Gordon Hayward became big and good enough to compete against the best high school players in Indiana. Despite the fact that he had grown to become a skilled high school player, he was still overlooked by some of the biggest basketball programs largely because it was only during his senior year when he broke out and because he was not as strong or explosively athletic as other prep prospects.

Brad Stevens, who was then the head coach of the Butler Bulldogs, gave Gordon Hayward a shot at a Division I scholarship in the mid-major Butler University, a school not known to produce the best basketball players. Hayward would star in Butler as his brand of smart all-around basketball was perfect for Stevens' system. With Brad Stevens preaching hard work and effort, Hayward became the perfect poster boy of the Butler Bulldogs' mantra of using work ethic and teamwork to get to the 2010 NCAA Finals.

Gordon Hayward would eventually find himself getting drafted by the Utah Jazz with the ninth overall pick of the 2010 NBA Draft to the dismay of some of the team's fans, who thought that they should have gotten a big man and that Hayward was not going to be a player that could help their team win. While it was true that the Butler product was still far from being a productive player, he brought with him the same work ethic and effort level to the NBA.

As seasons went by, it was clear that Gordon Hayward was improving his game and production. He went from a skinny boy band poster boy to a muscular grown man. His game changed as much as his body and face did. Gordon Hayward turned into a shot creator and attacker from being a pure shooter. He began to play the other aspects of the game at a high level and would eventually find himself getting named as an All-Star in 2017 because of how he was continuously improving his game and his team's level of success every season.

If there were one word to describe his impact to the game of basketball, it would be "evolution." Gordon Hayward can now be the poster boy of how a player can evolve and develop over time through hard work, patience, and discipline. Nobody gave the young Butler product his due. Nobody thought he had the potential to become a star someday. But Hayward took his time and showed significant improvements every season unlike other players, who would turn up one season but would suddenly regress a few years later.

With Gordon Hayward's development now complete, he has the opportunity to inspire fellow basketball enthusiasts and even those who are not even into basketball or sports to make the same evolution he did. No basketball player comes into the world with all the tools and skills he needs to become great. Some may end up becoming bigger and more athletically gifted than others. However, they also had to start from nothing at one point. Those with less potential and who are less physically gifted start from the same point as others do, but only through hard work and determination can they stay on par with those that have an elite level of talent. That was what Gordon Hayward did.

The player, whose height ceiling was 6'2", grew up as a guard not knowing he was going to be 6'8". Hayward worked on his craft and his body just as hard as one can in the NBA. From that moment that he nearly quit basketball, he never gave up on his desire to be a great NBA player. He was patient and never got frustrated with himself. As the mantra goes, "hard work beats talent when talent does not work hard." That is how Gordon Hayward can inspire the rest of the basketball world. His hard work towards evolving into a great player has become his impact not only on basketball or in the sporting world but in life itself in general.

Chapter 7: Legacy and Future

As a small forward, Gordon Hayward carries with him the legacy of elite small forwards that have been dominating the NBA as of late. While the NBA today may be considered a point guard's league, it has been the small forward spot that has become the game-changer for most championship teams. Championship teams today are led by dominant small forwards such as LeBron James, Kevin Durant, and Kawhi Leonard. Playing on a team looking to get back to the NBA Finals race, Gordon Hayward could be the next championship small forward in the league.

Hayward himself also continues the legacy of all-around small forwards that could score, shoot, rebound, make plays, and defend. When thinking about players with that kind of a skillset, one would think of Kevin Durant, Kawhi Leonard, and Paul George. However, Gordon Hayward has been establishing himself as an elite small forward that can do everything a team needs him to do. He is an elite shooter, versatile scorer, serviceable rebounder, all-around playmaker, and even a decent defender at the small forward spot. Considering that small forwards today are considered the Swiss Army knives of basketball, it is imperative for Hayward to continue to play like an all-around player for him to thrive in the NBA.

When Gordon Hayward left college to play in the NBA, he finished his playing years at Butler University as arguably the best basketball player the Bulldogs program has ever produced. Brad Stevens himself noted back then that he thought Hayward was good enough to make it to the NBA to become the first Butler player to be drafted in 60 years. However, Stevens never said anything about Hayward being good enough to become an All-Star. Not only is he the first Butler player to be drafted in 60 years but he is also the only one from that program that has made been named an NBA All-Star. Because of that, nobody could argue that he is the best basketball player that Butler University has ever produced.

Gordon Hayward also left behind a legacy in Utah as one of only 12 Jazz players to make an All-Star team. While Utah was never one of the more historically successful franchises and was never a team that became a hotbed for star talent, it has nonetheless been able to produce All-Star players such as Pete Maravich, Adrian Dantley, John Stockton, and Karl Malone.

Though Hayward has only made the All-Star team once in the seven years he spent in Utah, he has already established himself as one of the top 12 players in franchise history. As a small forward, he is up there with Adrian Dantley as the best the franchise has seen in that position. Had Gordon Hayward stayed longer with Utah, he could have solidified his hold as one of their best players by making more All-Star appearances and even by winning a title with that team.

Now a Celtic, Gordon Hayward carries with him a winning tradition that has spanned since the dawn of the NBA. The Boston Celtics do not settle with anything less than a championship considering that they are the winningest team in league history. That is the kind of legacy that Hayward now hopes to continue as he may be called upon by the Celtics to become one of the star leaders of a comparatively young team that is looking to make some noise in the coming seasons.

Still in the prime of his career, nobody can expect Hayward to slow down anytime soon. Gordon Hayward may even still be on the right track towards improving his game even further as the Boston Celtics expect more from him now that he has become an All-Star and now that he is playing in a system he is familiar with and with players that can help ease the burden off of him. He may even win a championship with the way the Celtics are built, though such a prospect is uncertain for any NBA team in the league. What is certain, however, for Hayward's future is that he will be an All-Star for several more seasons barring any serious injury. And when he finally hangs them up, he may end up as one of the best small forwards the league has ever seen.

Final Word/About the Author

I was born and raised in Norwalk, Connecticut. Growing up, I could often be found spending many nights watching basketball, soccer, and football matches with my father in the family living room. I love sports and everything that sports can embody. I believe that sports are one of most genuine forms of competition, heart, and determination. I write my works to learn more about influential athletes in the hopes that from my writing, you the reader can walk away inspired to put in an equal if not greater amount of hard work and perseverance to pursue your goals. If you enjoyed *Gordon Hayward: The Inspiring Story of One of Basketball's Star Forwards,* please leave a review! Also, you can read more of my works on *Roger Federer, Novak Djokovic, Andrew Luck, Rob Gronkowski, Brett Favre, Calvin Johnson, Drew Brees, J.J. Watt, Colin Kaepernick, Aaron Rodgers, Peyton Manning, Tom Brady, Russell Wilson, Michael Jordan, LeBron James, Kyrie Irving, Klay Thompson,*

Stephen Curry, Kevin Durant, Russell Westbrook, Anthony Davis, Chris Paul, Blake Griffin, Kobe Bryant, Joakim Noah, Scottie Pippen, Carmelo Anthony, Kevin Love, Grant Hill, Tracy McGrady, Vince Carter, Patrick Ewing, Karl Malone, Tony Parker, Allen Iverson, Hakeem Olajuwon, Reggie Miller, Michael Carter-Williams, John Wall, James Harden, Tim Duncan, Steve Nash, Draymond Green, Kawhi Leonard, Dwyane Wade, Ray Allen, Pau Gasol, Dirk Nowitzki, Jimmy Butler, Paul Pierce, Manu Ginobili, Pete Maravich, Larry Bird, Kyle Lowry, Jason Kidd, David Robinson, LaMarcus Aldridge, Derrick Rose, Paul George, Kevin Garnett, Chris Paul, Marc Gasol, Yao Ming, Al Horford, Amar'e Stoudemire, DeMar DeRozan, Isaiah Thomas, Kemba Walker and Chris Bosh in the Kindle Store. If you love basketball, check out my website at claytongeoffreys.com to join my exclusive list where I let you know about my latest books and give you lots of goodies.

Like what you read? Please leave a review!

I write because I love sharing the stories of influential athletes like Gordon Hayward with fantastic readers like you. My readers inspire me to write more so please do not hesitate to let me know what you thought by leaving a review! If you love books on life, basketball, or productivity, check out my website at claytongeoffreys.com to join my exclusive list where I let you know about my latest books. Aside from being the first to hear about my latest releases, you can also download a free copy of *33 Life Lessons: Success Principles, Career Advice & Habits of Successful People*. See you there!

Clayton

References

[i] Woods, Davis. "Before he was an NBA All-Star, Hayward was 'Stickboy' who nearly quit basketball". *Indy Star*. 26 January 2017. Web.

[ii] Garcia, Marlen. "Living a dream: Butler's Gordon Hayward mapped his success". *USA Today*. 1 April 2010. Web.

[iii] Kragthorpe, Kurt. "Jazz's Gordon Hayward: The brother from Brownsburg". *The Salt Lake Tribune.*. 25 February 2012. Web.

[iv] *Gordonhayward.com*. Web.

[v] *Draft Express*. Web.

[vi] Peterson, Tim. "2010 NBA Draft Results: Utah Jazz's Gordon Hayward Pick Brings out Boo Birds". *Bleacher Report*. 25 June 2010. Web.

[vii] Smith, Brian T. "Work just beginning for Jazz's Gordon Hayward during NBA lockout". *The Salt Lake Tribune*. 7 September 2011. Web.

[viii] Bailey, Andy. "Utah Jazz's Gordon Hayward Can Be the NBA's Next Point Forward". *Bleacher Report*. 6 October 2013. Web.

[ix] Gnessy, Jody. "Bulked-up Gordon Hayward looks to play with an edge this season for Utah Jazz". *Desert News.*. 1 October 2014. Web.

[x] Wasserman, Jonathan. "Gordon Hayward Proving He Belongs as an NBA Star". *Bleacher Report*. 12 November 2014. Web.

[xi] Jones, Tony. "Utah Jazz: Now fully developed, Gordon Hayward appears on his way to stardom". *The Salt Lake Tribune*. 4 November 2015. Web.

[xii] Mutoni, Marcel. "Kobe Bryant Tutored Gordon Hayward on Midrange Game". *Slam Online*. 15 December 2016. Web.

[xiii] Winderman, Ira. "Gordon Hayward says he left Miami Heat meeting ready to put jersey on". *Sun Sentinel*. 24 July 2017. Web.

[xiv] Genessy, Jody. "Gordon Hayward has 'excellent' meeting with Utah Jazz but remains undecided". *Deseret News*. 3 July 2017. Web.

[xv] Cato, Tim. "Gordon Hayward has 'excellent' meeting with Utah Jazz but remains undecided". *SB Nation*. 4 July 2017. Web.

[xvi] Hayward, Gordon. "The Case for Video Gaming". *The Players' Tribune*. 11 February 2016. Web.

Made in the USA
Las Vegas, NV
13 December 2020